CUT TO THE CHASE

'A fast-paced, punchy, down-to-earth and funny read that does what's on the label – it gets right to the heart of what matters.'
Jeff Lucas, author, speaker, broadcaster

'Funny, insightful, bold and more honest than a nun at confession. A must-read for men who want to understand themselves better and women who just want to understand men full stop.'
Jason Gardner, LICC

'Like two grizzly prophets these apple cart upsetters wander into your neat & tidy understanding of male belief and suggest a faith for blokes. Read it and weep manly tears in between bouts of raucous laughter.'
Dave Roberts, author and speaker

'Common sense is not that common. Nor is honesty, or speaking frankly in a way that actually encourages someone. So this is an uncommon book, because it does all these rare but so valuable things. The mixes of Christian faith, honesty, humour and vulnerability is a rare treat – for men and women alike!'
Revd Dr Martyn Atkins, Principal, Cliff College

'It's great to read raw material from some down-to-earth guys with no holds barred! It's about time us lads stopped chatting on a shallow level (although that's fun) and go deeper in our relationships with each other and God.'
Andy Hunter, DJ and recording artist as featured in *The Matrix: Reloaded* (trailer), *The Italian Job*, and *Alias*

'So many books today talk about a life that you can't relate to. Not this one! *Cut to the Chase* is about real life and how the reality of living that life with Jesus can impact your past, present and future! Read it NOW!'
Andy Rushworth, Nail the Truth Ministries

'I laughed, I cried, I felt offended (but quickly got over it!) and best of all felt challenged by the amazing honesty of some godly men who are prepared to talk openly about subjects that we so often brush under the carpet! I highly recommend you read it.'
Tim Owen, Genetik – The Tribe Academy

'A book that shocked me with its straight talking and honesty, yet had me laughing and crying all the way through – and it's supposedly only for men!'
Nancy Goudie, ngm

'In a world so twisted up in façade Christianity, we heartily recommend this book and urge you to be honest with yourself and Jesus as you read. Let your tears run onto your lap, let your laugh ring too loudly and may you meet Jesus again, or for the first time, as the one who knows you best and loves you the most.'

Bob and Ann Agee, good friends of Baz and Linda, Florida

'To most men, the word real is spelt "reel" and involves putting a maggot on the end of a line and waiting around for hours. The reality is the most men wait around for years to be REAL. In my dictionary the definition of real is, "The actual as opposed to the ideal." This book deals with the actual as opposed to the ideal, and in that has a power to transform cold, inactive men, sat waiting for hours, into alert, honest, actual men, aware of their own inadequacies but not prepared to let them stop them being the real men they actually are.'

Revd Andy Lenton, North-East Regional Youth Director of Serious4God

'Jackson, Gascoyne and friends have done it again! I find their honesty, integrity, and practicality refreshing. I recommend this book to every man who is tired of just "going through the motions" spiritually. This book knocks you out of your comfort zone and gets down to the real issues and struggles facing men today. As I read it I found myself challenged, convicted, and encouraged all at the same time.'

Dr Vaughan Stanley, Pastor, Westminster Presbyterian Church, Ft. Myers, Florida

'God developed a team of writers to come together and compile this very dangerous book. The book is a danger to every religious inclination in the church that broadcasts perfection and veils imperfection. Realise that if you read on you will likely ruin your religious front and destroy your desire to make everybody think you are something that you're really not.

'We all tend to operate on a basis of truth without honesty. Honesty demands the recognition of how far we tend to live from the truth. These pages express the sincere cooperation of truth and honesty as they collide together forming a strategic challenge that pierced my heart. Reading this work caused me to re-evaluate and increase my personal levels of accountability to be honest about and work more diligently to overcome my fleshly tendencies in life. We must be vulnerable if we want God to make us powerful.

'Let's face it. The church tends to exist in a real world without dealing with real issues. Reality shocks the church because so many Christian leaders preach sermons that answer questions nobody is asking. Reaching our world requires more than just a dream, for a dream without a strategy is just a fantasy. Thank God for courageous writers who have come together strategically, with a bold transparency for Christ!'

Pastor Lawrence Neisant, Destiny Christian Centre, International, Oklahoma

'*Cut to the Chase* is a book that is hard to put down, but there will be occasions when you will want to put it down; perhaps because it will be a little too raw and honest, maybe even offensive; but more likely because you will read something that so connects that you will have to take a time out to think, react, probably pray or even shed some tears. This is a strong book and if it does not take you forward in your journey with the Lord, I will be stunned. Read it – go on be good to yourself.'

Martin Scott, author of *Gaining Ground and Impacting the City*

'This is a great Christian self-help read. Jackson and Gascoyne show the reader that positive change is possible if they possess the penchant, planning and the persistence that is necessary and if they reach out to the Lord.'

John Richter, Senior Community Corrections Officer, Orlando County Jail, Florida

'These are two guys who are passionate about what it means to be a man of God, and with their fresh and exciting approach they will provoke and challenge us to answer the question 'What does it really mean to be a man of God?' This same question was posed to me recently by a 6th form lad, with no father around, who has committed his life to Jesus. This book is a refreshing, vulnerable, openhearted look at this question.'

Roy Crowne, National Director, YFC

'If you're an ordinary guy trying to follow Jesus and you want the raw truth, then read this book. If you want to laugh at yourself and say 'Ouch!' at the same time, Baz and Lee will have you take a long, loving look at men and the pressing issues we face with no short cuts.'

Sean Blomquist Pastor, Shelter Covenant Church, Concord, California

As I have become friends with Baz, I have been deeply moved by his passion for God and his uncompromising honesty. Being with Baz is not usually comfortable, but always challenging and lots of fun. I think that you'll find that this book affects you in the same way. There are few books available in the Christian press that combine this level of honesty and inspiration written in a very entertaining, down-to-earth way. Not one to read if you're easily offended, but if you are a man desperate for integrity and kingdom breakthrough in your life then you should not miss this book.

Revd Paul Maconochie, Senior Leader, St Thomas' Church, Sheffield

CUT TO THE CHASE

*Funny, Challenging and Straight Talking
for Men*

Lee Jackson, Baz Gascoyne and Friends

Authentic

MILTON KEYNES ● COLORADO SPRINGS ● HYDERABAD

Reprinted 2008

14 13 12 11 10 09 08   8 7 6 5 4 3 2

First published in 2006 by Authentic Media,
Authentic Media, 9 Holdom Avenue, Bletchley,
Milton Keynes, Bucks., MK1 1QR
1820 Jet Stream Drive, Colorado Springs, CO 80921, USA
OM Authentic Media, Medchal Road, Jeedimetla Village,
Secunderabad 500 055, A.P., India
www.authenticmedia.co.uk

Authentic Media is a division of IBS-STL U.K., limited by guarantee, with
its registered office at Kingstown Broadway, Carlisle, Cumbria CA3 0HA.
Registered in England & Wales No.1216232. Registered charity 270162

British Library Cataloguing in Publication Data
A catalogue record for this book is available from the British Library

ISBN 978–1–86024–544–2

Unless otherwise indicated, all Scriptural quotations are taken from
the New International Version, English Standard Version,
Contemporary English Version, New King James Version, The Message,
The Living Bible and The Amplified Bible.

Cover design by Sam Redwood
Typeset by Waverley Typesetters
Print management by Adare Carwin
Printed and bound by J. H. Haynes & Co., Sparkford

Dedication

Lee would like to dedicate the book to Jan, Ian, Marc and Kevin.

And Baz would like to dedicate the book to Ian, Andie, Jake, Imani and Neema and all at Bridge2Aid and to the people of Tanzania.

Contents

Acknowledgements

Baz would like say a huge thank you to the following people:

Valerie Marks from Sheffield Norton College who inspired me to learn and like reading and writing again.

To Lee Jackson, my friend, who has once again been patient with my slow typing but also encouraging as we have pursued this venture. I love you, son. Hold on to your dreams.

Northern Forum crew, big thanks for all your love and belief in me. The Hexthorpe retreat crew, thanks for helping me discover more about the intimacy of the Father.

Tim and John, my friends who have faithfully met with me for breakfast every three weeks to encourage, challenge and pray with me – it is much appreciated.

To Martyn Atkins for taking a risk – thank you, I really appreciate it and you very much.

Malcolm Down for his encouragement, James Davies for qauality editing and all at Authentic Media for all the work they have done to get this book in the hands of you the reader. Also Dave Roberts, Richard Herkes and Cathy Williams from Kingsway for being prepared to take a risk and encouragement with book 1.

For all the men who have contributed to this book, whether writing chapters, commendations or the foreword, you are all an inspiration to me but also to many more.

To John Richter from Orlando County Correcting Department – thank you for using the book in the Orange County Jail in Orlando, Florida. So pleased it has helped the young men you are working with. It was good to meet you in November and a huge privilege, also humbling, to speak to some of the young men you work with.

To all the people, men and women, who bought the last book and began the process of being real instead of 'fine'. And to all those who are going to read this book: don't settle for anything else but reality.

To the great people at the Eccles, who keep me sharp by their passion for Jesus, their love for each other and their communities and their amazing generosity. I am proud to be a member of the same church as you and serve you.

To Linda my wife, thank you for journeying with me so far in all that God has done for us and also for the love you have shown me in so many ways. I could not have done this with out your love. Thank you for 13 fantastic years together. I love you.

Finally, words cannot express the gratitude I have to you my Father God for all you have done, are doing and will do to make me the best Baz Gascoyne I can be. I love you.

Please continue to help me be more passionate, compassionate, and vulnerable with you and others as I learn more about what it really means to be a man of God, as I continue to be determined to follow your ways.

Lee would also like to thank:

Jeff Lucas, Pete Greig, Dave Roberts, and all those who have done commendations for us.

To all who took the risk of using our last book in men's groups or even inviting us to speak.

To the men and women who have kept me sane – Steve and Kathy, Linda H., Mike, Godfrey, Steve and Dawn, Jonathan and Rachel, Matt and Mel, Simon, Baz and Linda, Rob and Joy and Dr Ruth P.

Thanks to everyone at Authentic Media and also to Kingsway for starting us off on this journey.

To everyone at Leeds Faith in Schools – Claire, Scooter, Dan, Lynsey, Sarah, Chrissayburn.co.uk(!), Fiona, Mike and the rest of the clan and especially Christine – for your help with the manuscript – ta J. You are all a pleasure to work with.

To all the contributors, thank you for your patience, waiting for a publishing deal and with the endless emails and conversations with me and Baz.

To all at Dayspring – cheers!

To my Mum and Dad, Peter and Avril – I love you very much.

To anyone we've missed, we're really sorry – we are getting old and our minds are not what they … eh? What?

Special thanks to Duncan, Lenny and Justin – thanks for everything you are to me.

Extra special thanks and love to Clare, Rhea and Lauren – your cuteness and patience know no bounds.

Foreword

In those days spirits were brave, the stakes were
high, men were real men, women were real women
and small furry creatures from Alpha Centauri were
real small furry creatures from Alpha Centauri.

(Douglas Adams, *The Hitchhikers' Guide to the
Galaxy*, Macmillan, 1984)

Admittedly, there aren't as many books as there should
be for small furry creatures from Alpha Centauri. But for
women who want to be real women there is an entire
industry. And for men who want to be women there are
plenty of resources, too – especially if you happen to be
a Christian. But in this metrosexual age of football stars
prettier than your own wife, emotional intelligence at work
and liturgical dance workshops at church, there aren't
many books for ordinary bumbling blokes like you and me
who are neither macho nor metrosexual and who would
rather not wax their backs or wag a flag in worship.

Thank God, then, for the honesty and humour of this
new book from my good friends Baz and Lee. Some books
are like sermons. Some are more like songs. Some are so
boring they can make you yawn until your eyes swim
with tears. This one's like a long car journey on a wet day

with a good mate who's just a little bit manic because he's been drinking a lot of coffee. On road trips, stories get told at length and the conversation meanders between the superficial, the serious and the downright stupid. As traffic cones go whirring by, you sometimes stray into rare levels of honesty. There's the occasional inappropriate joke. The radio plays. And all the while it's raining and you're going somewhere together with a friend. It's just a whole lot easier to talk when you're not having to gaze into one another's big, ugly eyes. Miles easier.

What I'm saying is that I like the kinds of conversations you have on road trips and I really like this book because it's not like any other book on my bookshelf or by my toilet. Baz and Lee are the real deal – funny, friendly, passionate, faithful, honest, imperfect and kind. I've been down the pub with Lee. I've stayed in Baz's house on a number of occasions and he even sorted me tickets to go see Sheffield Wednesday play Liverpool (it was a few years ago now!). What's more, I can honestly say that Baz and Linda's love and support to my wife and me through some of the hardest months of our life was way beyond anything we had ever experienced before. People like that are the ones we should listen to in life.

Which brings me back to the content of this book … Men are good on camaraderie and this books models that beautifully by sharing the writing between a bunch of friends who are all trying to make sense of their faith in the real world and have never succumbed (as far as I know) to waxing their backs …

Men are also good on adventure and Steve Lowton's chapter on adopting a child from China is worth the cover price alone – not to mention Ian Wilson's story of being a dentist in Tanzania. And then there's Lee Saville's chapter on responding to Romania's orphans. Who says we can't change the world if we want to?

Personally, I think men are generally funnier than women. It's a controversial assertion admittedly but one that's only ever going to offend the kind of woman who doesn't know how to take a joke anyway. True to form, this book's got plenty of humour – not least the suggestion by Billy Prince (is that really his name?) that God speaks in a Geordie accent. Surely not ... I mean, everyone knows that God's posh, right?

Finally, I think men are pretty good at courage and this has to be one of the world's bravest books. How many authors have ever dared to let their wives and even their dad write chapters in their book – a book that also manages to talk about autism, retirement and porn? I rest my case.

So there you have it – a book that's courageous, funny, adventurous and as honest as a bunch of lads chatting on a long road trip while the radio plays. It's a book for men who don't want to be women any more than they want to be furry creatures from Alpha Centauri. It's a book for Christians who secretly like the fact that it was a ragtag gang of guys – a clumsy, argumentative bunch of oafs – that kick-started the church in the first place.

The first disciples showed very little inclination, as far as we can tell from detailed analysis of the evidence, towards getting their backs waxed. They wouldn't have been seen dead at a liturgical dance workshop when there was an entire world to be won for Jesus. They weren't perfect. We know that they sinned, they sometimes doubted and like men down the ages they occasionally got a bit competitive. They were real bumbling, hairy blokes and Jesus knew them, loved them and liked to call them his friends. This was the gang that started the church.

And they still found time to go fishing.

PETE GREIG
www.24-7prayer.com

On Lee and Baz

As this book is about plain speaking to you the reader, me and Baz didn't want to shy away from being dangerously honest ourselves, so ... what is one of the scariest things a man can do? Parachute? Cry in public? Meet his in-laws for the first time?

How about let your wife write a section of your book?! Let's face it, it's pretty scary to ask your wife to write something about you that thousands of other men will read, but hey, you take the rough with the smooth ...

On Lee

There are ugly things in all of us. My first thoughts when Lee said he wanted to write a second book were really cynical. I just thought it was a big ego trip for him. Like I said, ugly things right there. As we've talked together, I see it much differently now. The thing is really quite simple. Lee sees stuff around him and he thinks, 'I've got something to say about that. Maybe if someone heard it it would make a difference to them.'

I heard someone say once, in quite a negative way, that there are many people who could write a book, many people with something to say. I'm sure that this is true but the thing about Lee and Baz is that they have done it and they are doing it again. It really is very simple. Both these guys see stuff and say, 'I can make a difference there.' And they do.

A few weeks ago, Lee and I celebrated our eleventh wedding anniversary. My mom asked me how I felt about the 11 years. Well, I wouldn't choose to be anywhere else. There are lots of reasons why. Maybe because Lee can still surprise me, or because he takes the time to be romantic, or because he always encourages me and makes me feel good about myself in an insecure moment, or maybe just because he will sit and paint his kids' toenails with pink nail varnish. And just in case you think that Lee is some perfect husband, and that we float through life on a sweet-smelling boat of perfection and happiness, let's have a reality check. He's just an ordinary bloke who hates mornings, likes to be in control of the TV remote, has been known to show signs of grumpiness, gets mad with his kids and would struggle to cook something that didn't come out of a tin. (Am I being too honest now?) And sometimes he really makes me mad. Like I've already said, there are ugly things in all of us. The great thing is, life is not about being perfect. It's about doing the best you can with what you've been given. And just to finish my bit – Lee said to make sure I tell you that at 35 he still has skills on the turntables. (I always do as I'm told!)

CLARE

On Baz

'What's Baz like to live with?' or 'How do you cope?'. I've been asked those questions so many times over the years – usually by people who've been in a meeting where he's preached or shared prophetically and imagine the flamboyant exuberance is what he's like 100 per cent of the time.

Of course, those who know him well know that isn't the case. Yes, at times he's right there on the end of the extrovert scale – whether it's making people laugh, challenging and provoking, leading a battle cry, shouting at the enemy or crying at injustice. And yes, shouting at drivers who dare to cut him up! But at other times he's quiet, holding back, thoughtful, worried about the impression he's giving and whether he's said the right thing and trying not to lead in case it appears that he's hogging the show.

Why am I saying all this? Because when I was asked to write something about Baz I felt it was important to present a true picture. Well, as true a picture as it's possible for a wife to present about her husband!

Those of you reading this book who know Baz, know what he's like – warts and all. But for those of you who don't, it's easy to imagine that someone who's written a book is pretty special: put them on a pedestal, read the stories and assume they all happen within a short space of time resulting in a constant, amazing, rollercoaster ride of spiritual experiences.

I'm writing this in Tanzania, and in the first few days of preaching in a new culture, I saw Baz's insecurities shutting him down, preaching with a hesitancy I hadn't seen for a while; and then the encouragement of the team helped him bounce back and adjust, confident that people accepted him. Is he insecure? Of course. Needing encouragement and affirmation? Of course. Fearless for his God? Absolutely.

So, back to the original question: what is Baz like to live with? Well, I realised on our honeymoon life was never going to be boring. We were on a cliff top in Malta, and I was admiring the crashing waves from a good few feet back from the cliff, whilst Baz was peering over the cliff edge saying 'come close and see, its fantastic'. Eventually, I dared to step forward to the edge, holding tightly onto Baz, and discovered the view from there was ten times as fantastic as the one I had been enjoying from my safe spot. Life on the edge, now there's a phrase I would have to get used to.

And all you guys who think being a real man, strong and tough guy, means you can't share your feelings, think again. Baz is the most romantic man I know. Grand gestures of stretch limousines and surprise wedding anniversary trips to New York are all good, but so are the smaller touches – hiding cards and love notes around the house when he goes away, running my bath for me and lighting the candles, leaving a lemon on my desk at work when I had a cold!

And you will have noticed if you have read any of the book, a vulnerability that is refreshing and scary depending on your perspective. The first time I met Baz, he came into a meeting where I worked to speak to a team of Christian community development workers. His friend had been killed in a motorbike accident, and Baz shared how he was feeling, encouraged us to be real with God about things going on in our lives and left to cry in his office. As a 'let's keep it together' kind of girl this was a shock – instrumental in me seeking help to sort out some issues in my life.

And just in case you think I've mistaken him for some kind of saint, he can be incredibly frustrating – letting his insecurities hold him back at times, not believing in himself the way he should, impatient when things aren't moving quick enough or when he's focused, highly embarrassing when he gives people prophetic words in restaurants (spot me running to the toilet?) and, horror of horrors, pretty useless at DIY!

But there's one thing you'll learn from Baz, and you'll either love it or you'll hate it. Absolute, genuine, toe-curling honesty. Honesty with himself. Honesty with others. And honesty with God. So I recommend this book, not just because Baz is my husband and Lee a friend, but because I think we all need a bit more raw honesty and passion for God in our lives and, if nothing else, I think this book will give that. Enjoy!

LINDA

'cut to the chase'

The phrase 'cut to the chase' developed from cinema terminology, where it referred to the act of switching from a less action-packed scene to a more exciting sequence ... within the past 15 years or so, 'cut to the chase' has come to be used outside of the film industry with the figurative meaning of 'get to the point'.

[Source: Mark Israel, http://alt-usage-english.org/, 'phrase origins', 'cut to the chase']

Why spend a whole book padding out a single idea like a lot of Christian books? Let's cut to the chase and rock the boat – not get another warm bath!

Visit us www.leeandbaz.com

Introduction

If you look for men's books on Amazon.com there are 22,034 different books about, or for, men, so what makes this one different? Simple really, this one is written by normal men and it is very honest.

It won't contain the best grammar you've ever read but it will deliver a raw honesty. At no point in this book do I, Baz, or anyone else who has written for us, want to pretend that we have made it. We don't want to preach or tell anyone how they should live their life, we just want to share where we have been, some of the mistakes and some of the joys that we have found so far.

When one of the biggest role models in the world, David Beckham, just after the birth of his first child Brooklyn says, 'I would like Brooklyn to be christened but I don't know what religion yet', you know we are in trouble! Lowell Shepherd has written: 'I am amazed at how many young men I meet who are nice ... Very much in touch with their intuition and emotions but boring. They have no drive. When pressed, they talk about dreams but have little determination to turn fantasy into reality.'[1]

Phil Wall says that in many university Christian Unions today, it is hard to find young men who will take responsibility because of a crisis in confidence. 'They are not sure how to play their role in situations of mutual leadership and submission,' he says. Of the binge drinking and violence we see on the streets, he adds, 'If genuine masculinity does not find a way to be expressed and affirmed, then it will find a dysfunctional expression.'

Phil Wall sees the macho culture as evidence that these people have no context in which to express genuine masculinity. A culture is crying out for a difference.[2]

Books addressing this are not easy to write because you have to share a lot of your life and a lot of mistakes that perhaps some authors would try to hide. It was refreshing to read that just before *The Lord of the Rings* was published, the author J.R.R. Tolkien said, 'I have exposed my heart and allowed it to be shot at.'

It was encouraging that even when writing fiction, Tolkien felt that he had bared his soul and also thought that what he had written wasn't particularly of much use! You know that he was open to be shot at and I guess that's what happened to us with our first men's book, *Dead Men Walking*.

Dead Men Walking received one specific complaint from a significant Christian leader in the UK[3] asking why someone would publish something as honest as this. So we ruffled a few feathers, but I think that is probably what we were meant to do. But we are not writing to shock. What we want to do is to be honest. Perhaps that church leader, and some other men in the UK, just aren't able to handle the fact that we are a little bit more honest than what we have all been used to. But we need this honesty to survive. Christian Viewpoint for Men,[4] a Christian men's organisation that puts on conferences, recently extrapolated from Christian research stats the percentage of men in church attendance figures. In 1978 the number of men attending church had fallen to 45 per cent. And if the decline continues further, by 2021 men will make up only 10 per cent of churchgoers!

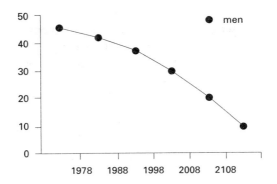

This is a serious situation and we have to ask ourselves why it is happening. We hope this book and website will help.

We hope the book encourages you and / or really annoys you! What is the point of writing a book that nobody remembers? We don't do bland.

Notes

1. Lowell Sheppard, *Boys Becoming Men*, Authentic Lifestyle, 2002.
2. These quotes are taken from the article by Nathaniel Lewis from http://www.eauk.org/contentmanager/Content/idea/2004-07/masculinity.cfm
3. We genuinely don't know who this was but Baz has spent £35,000 of his own money trying to find out.
4. Christian viewpoint for men www.cvmen.org.uk

Life is not the amount of breaths you take, but the moments that take your breath away

(From the film *Hitch*, Columbia Pictures, 2005, with Will Smith)

1

General Lee and Baz

Obviously there are going to be some generalisations that take place. You'll have to give us a little bit of licence for that. We have tried to trace all quotes used as best we can but please bear with us in slight generalisations!

Some have said that there is a crisis of leadership in the church and I think there is a crisis of manhood as well. It is fair to say that since our last book, we realised that when men see faith lived out in a real and honest way then other men get it! A good friend of mine read the last book and he took major steps forward. I had the opportunity to pray with him and he gave his life to God, which was a bit of a shock to me, but it was just the fact that he saw something real and he got it. It made sense to him for the first time.

> Some men are born mediocre, some men achieve mediocrity, and some men have mediocrity thrust upon them.
>
> (Joseph Heller, *Catch-22*, Vintage, 2005)

Cheeky Monk

Recently on BBC television there was a documentary called *The Monastery* in which five men from different walks of

1

life came to live in the monastery at Worth in the UK for 40
days. One of the men, Tony Burke, gave an account of his
story there. He said, 'My religious background is simple,
I just haven't got one.'

At the end of the 40 days, Tony received a blessing from
one of the monks and he had a real experience of God. This
40 days' experience of living in a place of faith with real
men made him open to spirituality. When he first went to
the monastery, he thought that God didn't exist, church
was for old people who smelt of wee, priests were just
running from life and theologians were on a meal ticket
attempting to answer the unanswerable question of the
existence of God, and they would thrash it out until they
retired to Spain. Pretty strong words but somehow still he
managed to find real faith through meeting these guys in
the monastery.

Tony says that his world-view has changed; he says
he is not sure he is ready to go to church services yet,
and doesn't label himself as a Christian, but that he has
definitely changed his life. He says clearly that God
exists.

When I hear stories like this it encourages me because
as we give permission, or as we fight for permission, to live
out our Christian lives in a manly way, it really changes
the world and the people around us.

Stubborn

Sometimes it's just about being stubborn with our faith and
church and persevering. My favourite basketball player
was a guy called John Starks who played for New York
Knicks. He did one of the best dunks of all time over the top
of Michael Jordan and he was only 6'2"! His coach, Dave
Checkett, said about John Starks, 'I have seen some players
come and go who have had more talent, but they didn't

play as hard, they didn't work as hard and they didn't care as much as John did.' That's what we want to do. Let's be full on, let's do what we can, have a real laugh along the way and let's put our faith into action and, as men, learn what it is to follow God in a non-religious way.

> Boys will be boys, and so will a lot of middle-aged men.
>
> (Kin Hubbard (1868–1930))

Lonely

I travelled to Norway to DJ at a gig a couple of years ago and I met a guy there who was the organiser of the event. He spent a bit of time showing me around Norway in the winter – an amazing place! As we talked, I realised that this guy was trying to follow God but he was pretty lonely in his church. The church was religious and he found going there very difficult. As he heard more about my book, he really started to cry out for some reality; he was desperate in his country, and his town, to find other guys he could hang out with. There is still a need out there, a need for reality and honesty – let's hope we can get to people before they disappear.

So what are we all about?

Well, men are complicated creatures, there is no doubt about that. Dave Barry in his article from www.thisisawar.com says 'men went to the moon but guys invented mooning!'

Dave goes on to say that perhaps men haven't really been well represented over the years because we are rubbish at writing things down. He says that on the whole women spend a lot of time writing thank-you notes but men spend most of their time scratching their bits! He even goes on to say, 'I wonder whether the *Titanic* would have sunk if the Captain wasn't busy at the time readjusting his bits and bobs!' Well, it's complicated down there!

Chris Rock says that men only want three things: peace and quiet, the big chicken leg and the remote control. That all seems pretty simple.

Is that who we really are? What about directions? There is absolutely no doubt that GPS navigation systems were invented for men. Women seem to have intuition to get them to places, but men can be totally lost in the middle of the countryside and will still be too proud to ask for directions. GPS has certainly sorted my life out a few times, that's for sure. Yet, strangely, on my GPS it has a woman's voice which calmly tells me to 'turn left in three tenths of a mile' so even when we do need directions, the GPS software people are having a laugh at us, putting a female voice on it!

> I stand by all the misstatements that I've made.
>
> (Dan Quayle)

Ignore

You just wonder why some guys don't want to deal with who they are. In particular, some Christian guys really don't want to understand what it is to be a man and deal with some of the issues. The fun thing about our last book was that it was ignored by many people. There are some major men's conferences in the UK and me and Baz don't get invited to speak. There are not that many books written by Christian men and there is the off chance that our book was just rubbish(!) but you realise that in certain circles and denominations, certain men's organisations, people have their own speakers and perhaps they just don't want people who are going to be honest. It is movements like www.xxxchurch.com that have really kept my faith in this whole thing, where guys are willing to deal with issues that no one else will talk about. That's exactly what we want to do here. I got tapes from a recent men's conference in the UK and *none* of the teaching was related to any of the inner struggles that men have. It was all inspirational stuff about 'go for it' and 'deal with your past' a bit and 'go for it' and 'God loves you', yet not actually dealing with the nitty-gritty of being totally honest in a completely male environment. It was just weird! Why is that? I'm afraid to say that it is probably because a leader can only take people as far as they have been themselves. A scary thought.

But before you think me and Baz are outside the church slagging people off, you need to know that Baz leads a church and I am an active member of my church. You can go to semi-traditional church and be an agitator as well – maybe that's who we were called to be. Standing outside the church taking the rip may be funny but it isn't half as powerful and becomes empty very quickly. (Although those kind of voices should still be heard.)

At last!

In the film *Jerry McGuire*,[1] Jerry, a sports agent, stays up one night and decides to write a paper which explains why he got into his industry in the first place. It is an industry which has become dominated by money rather than caring for people. In the middle of the night, Jerry gets out his laptop and writes this paper (which he admits is a bit 'touchy feely') and he calls it, 'The things that we think but do not say'. (I guess that's how we sometimes felt, which is why we decided to say those things in this book!) After he has written the paper, Jerry McGuire says, 'I feel like I have started my life.' That's what it felt like for me a few years ago after trying to find, for so long, Christian men who I could appreciate, who I could respect and who I could follow. It was only a few years ago when I started meeting guys like that. I thought, 'Yes, I have started my life now and I know what it is to be a man!'

Men who never get carried away should be.

(Malcolm Forbes (1919–90))

Chuffin' folk music!

In the late eighties I was mad on hip hop. Public Enemy were a particular favourite of mine. When we used to go to Greenbelt (a Christian arts festival), we used to bring the biggest stereo that we could find and after adding extra speakers to it we put the stereo on a trolley and walked around with Public Enemy or Run DMC blasting out. It's funny but all the bands that we stopped to listen to were 'guitar driven'. We found something in 'secular' hip hop that we just couldn't find in the Christian world at that point. There was a lot of folk guitar music but instead the power, purpose and radicalism of Public Enemy and others from the late eighties was attractive. They had hardcore beats with strong lyrics about being a man and standing up for what you believe in – very attractive to a teenage boy. As we went around the festival, we loved the people and yet the music just seemed weak, folk-driven, guitar stuff which just didn't do anything for us. We were really desperate for something different. A couple of years later we formed our own hip hop group and became the first Christian rap group in the UK. I have been a DJ ever since.

Depth

There is a rumour that Robin Williams, Steve Martin, Billy Connolly and loads of other famous comedians meet up once in a while and spend a weekend together laughing, drinking and whatever. I always find it quite amazing that all these key comics, in order to be inspired, would hang out once in a while just for a bit of sanity with each other. I guess that once they'd been together it would spur them on for a while. That is exactly what I have found at the Evangelist conference and other conferences where I meet up with my friends. We can be honest with each other, get to God, and occasionally break wind together, and sometimes even light it!

So here we go ...

Me and Baz are both normal (ish!) blokes. We both love a bit of sport, play football and basketball. Baz is a church leader, evangelist and a wannabe comedian! I am a schools worker, a veteran DJ and a dad. No easy answers here, loads of real life stories, but above all an honest, real approach that will pull *very* few punches. No weird theories just real life lessons. Are you up for it? If you are easily offended, put this down now and go read 'have a lovely warm bath with vague spiritual quotes' available at your local bookshop.

> I don't want any yes-men around me. I want everybody to tell me the truth even if it costs them their jobs.
>
> (Samuel Goldwyn (1882–1974))

For more info and resources, including chapters we couldn't fit in this book, see www.leeandbaz.com.

Notes

[1] *Jerry McGuire*, TriStar Pictures Inc, 1996.

We need more 'jackass' Christianity.

(Steve Chalke)

2

Caves and Sheds

LEE JACKSON

People give you strange looks when they hear that you are writing a book, especially if you are writing about men! And as my friends got to realise that I wasn't actually taking the rip and I was genuinely writing a book, and now a second book, on men they started giving me strange presents. One of my favourites was *The Bluffer's Guide to Men*[1] – a small paperback allowing people to try and understand everything you need to know about being a man or talking to men. It is a short book!

My mam also found one of my primary school books where, along with a few sketchy teachers' comments, I get an excellent mark for a story where I talked in some length about how I killed my teacher. I was young.

> He's turned his life around. He used to be depressed and miserable. Now he's miserable and depressed.
>
> (David Frost)

But the best so far is Gordon Thorburn's book *Men and Sheds*. It's a fascinating book for which Gordon and his photographer (who incidentally is a woman), travelled all over the UK looking at men and, surprisingly, their sheds. Everything from an astronomer's observatory, a UFO investigator and a suffragan bishop of the Church of England who used his shed as a chapel! This little book gives us a glimpse into that secret part of a man's life – his shed!

'Shed' comes from the Anglo-Saxon for 'shade', 'scead', pronounced 'shay-ud' which is how they still say it in certain northern districts of England. 'Scead' means partial darkness or comparative obscurity ... That is what sheds are all about. The quiet life, a hiding place.

As I thumbed through this bizarre book of British eccentrics, my mind jumped to the groundbreaking relationship book – *Men are from Mars, Women are from Venus*.[2] One of the memorable things from this book is John Gray talking about a man and his cave (or perhaps a man and his shed). There are definitely a lot of parallels between men and sheds, and men and caves.

Why?

John Gray says a man goes into his cave or becomes quiet for a variety of reasons.

1. He needs to think about a problem and find a practical solution to the problem.
2. He doesn't have an answer to a question or a problem.
3. He needs to be alone to cool off, to find his control again.
4. He needs to find himself ... Whenever they get too close, so as to lose themselves, alarm bells go off and they are on their way into their cave ...

John Gray goes on to say that 'men go into their caves in the same way that women talk'. It is a place where we regain some strength and understand who we are as men and women.

Scary

One of the important things that women learn when dealing with men is that the cave (or perhaps shed) is for men only, and in this politically correct age it is rather uncomfortable to say it, but women are not allowed in sheds and certainly will never be allowed in a man's cave. If they venture in by accident they may regret it, particularly if the cave has got a 'man shrine'[3] in it!

The full Monty

Most of us are not quite eccentric enough to actually have our own 'man shed' in the back garden. Maybe we might use our shed occasionally, like in the heartbreaking scene from the movie *The Full Monty*[4] when Mark Addy's character, Dave, who is concerned about his weight, goes into the shed and wraps cling film around his stomach while eating a Mars bar, hoping that the weight will disappear. We all need space, no doubt, and sometimes we really hope for a bit of peace and quiet, especially those of us that have young families. It doesn't mean we don't love them or we don't like them. It just means that we all need space, time to think and for some of us, time to pray as well.

There is a very fine line between 'a hobby' and a 'mental illness'

So we don't all have a collection of milk bottles like Ken, who apparently spends most of his time embarrassing his wife by stopping on the A1 and looking in hedgerows for milk bottles thrown away by lorry drivers many years ago!

But it is definitely fair to say that it is easy for us to get lost in our sheds (or our caves). For some people, it could be easy to spend their whole life hiding in there. I know that life is difficult sometimes, and we do need to get away from it all, but a lot of the time we need to tread this fine line between hobbies and mental illness very carefully. Maybe sometimes when we do get stuck in our 'sheds', we need to give permission for other blokes to join us or even for other blokes to kick us out of the shed! Maybe we should talk to God a little bit more as well instead of bottling everything up. (No reference to milk intended!) I have met a lot of men who are not happy with life but somehow think that it is best not to deal with it; a sad place to be. When you start thinking like that you move into 'existing' rather than 'living' and that is a dangerous state to be in. I'm pretty sure Jesus didn't come so that we could just exist, get through it, scrape by and be a bit miserable.

> Most of the time I don't have much fun. The rest of the time I don't have any fun at all.
>
> (Woody Allen)

A sh(ar)ed moment

Sometimes you get a rare glimpse of a private moment, a cave or shed moment, if you like. Over the last few years, the female artist Sam Taylor-Wood has developed a project inviting A-list actors from Hollywood to break down and cry in front of her camera. She said that a few of these actors did fake it, but some of them were very genuine. It took between five minutes and several hours for these men to cry, but Sam definitely viewed a few shed moments there, and she even said herself that it felt a bit odd: 'It's really hard to be in a room with a grown man crying especially if you are responsible for it.' Sam had a unique opportunity to see something of a rarity – a man on his own crying, a cave moment, a shed moment. It is quite rare for a woman to see that and something which I'm sure has profoundly affected her life and work.

You see, John Gray's book, *The Bluffer's Guide to Men*, and many of the endless emails that I get sent, with so-called 'hilarious men's quotes' in them, seem to forget one thing, and that is the presumption that men don't change and that men are just going to be like they are, for ever.

There is a large part of us that won't change – particularly our strengths and gifts. But if we know God, we are being changed all the time, hopefully becoming more like Jesus every day. We *can* change. I've seen loads of my friends change, some of them dramatically. I have changed, too. It's a lie to think that we can't change and we should just accept ourselves (the *Men Behaving Badly* syndrome). Sometimes, we have to get out of our caves and our sheds to actually do something about it.

For groups and you …

- Where is your shed? (And don't say your back garden!)
- Is your shed a habit?
- Why do men need time to themselves? Do women, too?
- Does God hang out in your shed as well?
- Is your shed healthy? Does it have a shrine?!

P.S. While I was writing notes for this chapter, Clare saw them on the desk and wrote me a little note to share with you lads! She wrote, 'Sometimes women go into their own sheds as well but they have cosy armchairs and hot chocolate.'

Notes

[1] Antony Mason, *The Bluffer's Guide to Men*, Oval Books, 1999.
[2] John Gray, *Men are from Mars, Women are from Venus*, Harper Collins, 2002. Reprinted by permission of HarperCollins Publishers Ltd © John Gray.
[3] Some men go beyond sheds and caves and build shrines to their footy team, pin up or hobby!
[4] *The Full Monty*, Fox Searchlight Pictures, 1997.

Women have colds, men have flu.

3

24771134

BAZ GASCOYNE

Imagine if you will that Sir Alan Sugar or Donald Trump is interviewing a prospective apprentice for one of their companies. They have nearly finished the interview and the last question before making the decision to employ or not is, 'Tell me something interesting about yourself.' What would they do, do you think, if the response was one of the following? 'Well, I can eat 2lb of metal a day and so far I have eaten 18 bicycles, 15 supermarket trolleys, 7 TV sets, 6 chandeliers, a low calorie Cessna light aircraft and a computer' or 'I have walked 70.16 miles while balancing a milk bottle on my head taking me 18 hours and 46 minutes' or 'I once spat a cherry stone 88'5½", which is approximately 26.96 metres'. (Factfile by Dick Millingham taken from the *Mail on Sunday*, 29 January 1995.)

It would be wonderful to see either man speechless as they listened in disbelief to the achievements of the candidate. For Michel Lotito, Ashrita Furman or Horst Otrmann, these are genuine claims to fame. I would love to ask them how they discovered they can eat metal, balance a milk bottle on their head and walk for so long, or spit a cherry stone so far.

I am always intrigued by what lengths men and women will go to achieve some amazing or not so amazing feat. Is it the 'rush' of being the first or the best at something, regardless of what it is? Is it because we have a fear of not feeling important or because we long to be remembered after we die?

The dictionary informs us that identity is: 'The collective aspect of the set of characteristics by which a thing is definitively recognisable or known. The personality of an individual regarded as a persisting entity.' And identity crisis is: 'Psychology, a period of disorientation and anxiety resulting from difficulties experienced in resolving personal conflicts, adjusting to social demands and pressures of our lives.'

Who are you? This is a question often asked by one person of another but also frequently asked of ourselves.

From an early age, a child takes on an identity through the name they are given by their parents and who friends and relatives think the child looks like. As that child grows up, society continues to help build a positive or negative identity for him or her.

At school our identity is formed through our ability in the classroom or on the playing field. Once we leave school, our identity is given by a number, e.g. our National Insurance number, also whether we go to college or university or get a job. Most men are desperate to feel valued, appreciated and important and try and find this in what they do.

> Males are suffering a lost sense of identity.
>
> (Dr Myles Munroe, *Understanding the Purpose and Power of Men*, Whitaker House, 2001)

When I joined the army, my name was no longer my main identity but my army number was. It took me nearly two weeks to remember and recite it on request: '24771134, Sir'. It's over 20 years since I had my very short spell in the 11th Regiment of The Royal Signals, Number 3 troop at Helles Barracks at Catterick (and it was Hell on earth believe me). The physical side I loved but constantly being bullied for my faith in God eventually got the better of me when I decided turning the other cheek was not good enough and I laid down the fivefold ministry!

It is so easy to allow ourselves to fall into the trap of our identity being built on our job title or position or what we own. Dr Neil Anderson in his book, *Victory Over Darkness*, tells us in the first chapter how he loves asking the question 'Who are you?' He explains that he might answer 'Neil Anderson'.

> 'No, that's your name. Who are you?'
> 'Oh, I'm a seminary professor.'
> 'No, that's what you do.'
> 'I'm an American.'
> 'That's where you live.'
> 'I'm an evangelical.'
> 'That's your denominational preference.'
>
> (Dr Neil Anderson, *Victory Over Darkness*,
> Monarch Publications, 2002)

All my life I have struggled with my identity. At junior school I was known as the boy who could run fast, count quickly on his fingers and whose mam and dad didn't live together. During senior school, the boy who could still run fast, couldn't count and was beginning to get grey hairs on his head. After school, I was known as the one who could not hold down a job for too long and who had a big mouth which got him into trouble often.

When, at the age of 17½, I became a Christian, my identity was changed immediately by my peers. I was now known as 'Bible Basher Baz' or 'Holy Joe'.

When friends from our church introduce me to some of their friends I make sure they introduce me as their mate Baz and not as the 'Senior Pastor' or 'Leader' of the church. I am just one of them whose role happens to be a leader of the church. No better than anyone else.

Why do we love to put people in a box and have everything wrapped and signed? Comparing our children with our friends' children, asking certain questions of people we meet so we can pigeon-hole them in our mind and keep everything neat and tidy. I love messing up those neat pigeon-holes!

I was a very insecure young man before I became a Christian and realise that I am now an insecure older man in many ways. Why? Well, for various reasons. First, because I became aware of the things in my life that needed to change in order for me to become more like the man God wanted me to be.

Secondly, because I often felt I was failing to live to the standard the church expected of me. Not God but the church.

Thirdly, the more I got involved with the church and began to develop in areas of leadership, I became aware of how insecure most church leaders are, especially when they gather together with other male leaders. Men – we behave like a bunch of fat-heads worrying about how big each others churches are and how mine compares with yours. It used to be the size of our 'willies' we were worried about but now it's churches. The funny thing is, it is done in such a polite way. 'How's the church going Baz?' (meaning 'How big is it now?') with a quiet prayer being offered up simultaneously 'Please God don't let it be as big as mine.' I remember about two years after we started the Eccles (the church I co-lead), I was introduced to a group of other leaders in the following way: 'This is

Baz who leads a *small* church.' Could he really be saying, 'Mine is bigger than yours'? When I responded, 'Actually we've grown to about seventy people,' his face was a picture. Green with envy. I put him out of his misery ten minutes later when I confessed to kidding about the numbers we were getting, but the response had said it all.

> As long as I am constantly concerned about what I ought to say and think, do or feel, I am still the victim of my surroundings and not liberated. But when I can accept my identity from God and allow him to be the centre of my life, I am liberated from compulsion and can move without restraints.
>
> (Henri J. M. Nouwen, http://open-mind. org/SP/Quotes.htm)

I love being in the company of other men where I know there is no pressure to try and impress but I can totally be myself, where it's OK to question some aspects of church or the Bible knowing I am in a safe place to air these feelings and thoughts rather than worrying about what I say in case it will be used in evidence against me.

When seven Russian crew members were rescued from their mini submarine that was entangled in a fishing net over 600 feet down on the seabed their response was real. The rescuers and those rescued, as well as reporters, were ecstatic as the submarine came up to the surface, the hatch was opened and out came the Russian sailors. 'It would be wrong for me to say grown men didn't cry. I assure you lots of grown men cried that day,' remarked Commander Ian Riches who led the British rescue team being interviewed on BBC Radio 4 news, 9 August 2005.

All God is asking of you, the person who is reading this chapter, is to be yourself. You and I will not find security that will last apart from in God. How do you receive this?

First, by being honest enough to say that in the past your identity has been in what you do, what you own, what others think, which has never really brought you contentment.

> I see many men walking around in midlife with a sense of yearning for things that they can't get from their wives and can't get from their jobs and can't pull from inside themselves. Having listened to thousands of stories in workshops around the world, I'm convinced what the men are missing is a sense of their own identity: a very primitive and very deep sense of validation that passes from father to son.
>
> (Gordon Dalby, *Sons of the Father*, Kingsway Communications, 1996)

Secondly, by recognising that our true identity comes from our heavenly Dad, and learning what he says about us: that I am a friend of Jesus (Jn. 15:13–15); that he chose me (Jn. 15:16); I am a son of God (Gal. 3:26; 4:6; Rom. 8:14,15). By allowing my identity in God to develop daily, reassures me that I am not a number but a child of his; that he knows my name personally. I am Baz and he is Dad.

Questions

- Who are you?
- Do you worry about your identity?
- What, or who, shapes your identity?
- Is God a distant creator or a close and loving Father who calls you his son?
- Who are the people that you can be yourself with and are you developing these friendships?

Since Jesus went through everything you're going through and more, learn to think like him. Think of your sufferings as a weaning from that old sinful habit of always expecting to get your own way. Then you'll be able to live out your days free to pursue what God wants instead of being tyrannised by what you want.

(1 Pet. 4:1,2, The Message)

4

The Parable of the Nice Samaritan

MATT PAGE

A man was going down from Jerusalem to Jericho, when he fell into the hands of robbers. They stripped him of his clothes, beat him and went away, leaving him half-dead.

A priest happened to be going down the same road, and when he saw the man, he passed by on the other side. So, too, a Levite, when he came to the place and saw him, passed by on the other side.

But a Christian, as he travelled, came where the man was; and when he saw him, he took pity on him. He was about to go and offer him some help when he thought to himself, 'Hang on, this guy might not actually want my help, he might be OK. Those two guys walking ahead a bit further up the road might be on the way to fetch help. The last thing he would want is somebody else sticking their nose in and making things worse for the poor bloke. I don't want to offend him by offering my help. Besides, I have a prayer meeting that I'm already five minutes late for.'

So the Christian smiled at the man and headed on to his meeting. And whilst he was there, he thanked God that although he hadn't really made much of a difference to the world today, at least he hadn't offended anyone.

www.biblefilms.blogspot.com

We are all history makers, it is just that we either make good history or bad history.

5

Christian Comedy?

JOHN ARCHER

> To get a job where the only thing you have to do in your career is to make people laugh – well, it's the best job in the world!
>
> (Ronnie Barker)

People often refer to me as a 'Christian comedy magician' – a strange title if ever there was one. I prefer to be known as a 'comedy magician' who is a Christian, but people only end up saying, 'Ah right, I've never met a 'Christian comedy magician' before ... Duh! It's too subtle for some people to grasp. However, that's not the point so let's move on before I get angry ...

I'd like to have a look at comedy in a Christian context. I know the 'magic' aspect of my title may be slightly more tempting for the reader, but I haven't got the space at this time to address that little hot potato, which seems to upset the odd few Christians who (in my opinion) are a little too superstitious for their own good. So let's move on, before I get angry, again.

Two things I'd like to look at in this chapter are: Is comedy 'Christian'? And if it is, how should Christians use it?

Is comedy 'Christian'?

Laughter and comedy has often been frowned upon by serious thinkers of the past – whether philosophers or theologians – as unseemly, frivolous, an abdication of reason or, worse, a diabolical temptation. But where did they get this thinking? Is the Bible funny? Do we ever read of Jesus laughing? The answer to that last question is no. In fact the only time laughing is mentioned in the New Testament is when we read about the mourners in the house of Jairus who laugh at Jesus for saying that an evidently dead child is alive (see Mt. 9:24) – a reasonable reaction I suppose. Just because there is no mention of Jesus laughing in the Bible does not of course prove that he didn't laugh. He probably drank milk and fell over lots of times, certainly when he was a child, but no mention is made of either of those. (I don't think.)

I find it difficult to believe that Jesus was devoid of a sense of humour. 'People liked Christ,' said Beppe Grillo, one of Italy's leading satirical comedians. 'If he had been too serious a man he wouldn't have had such a following.' It's true, one only has to observe Jesus' behaviour and listen to his parables to be hit in the face by his sense of humour. He shared meals with outcasts and sinners, announced that prostitutes would go before the pious into heaven and his first miracle was to change water into wine. He reversed accepted values with irony and humour. I can't imagine a serious guy getting away with that, even if he was God. Look at the way he handled James and John, two hot-tempered disciples who at one time would have smitten people with fire (given the chance). They asked Jesus if they could have a special place in Heaven for goodness sake. What did he nickname them? He called them the 'Sons of Thunder' ... now that is funny. I think we can safely assume that doing what he did and hanging around with twelve rough-cut fishermen, he must have had a keen sense of humour.

We also read some funny things in the Bible, like the fate of the aptly named Eutychus ('You teach us'?), who was killed by a boring sermon but fortunately revived by the preacher (Acts 20:7–12). I think that happened to me once! Or the example of a disciple who, referring to Jesus' home town, asked: 'How could anything good ever come from Nazareth?' (Jn. 1:46). There is certainly more than a hint of sarcasm creeping in there. Another classic example of humour is in Luke's gospel, when Zacchaeus, a short man and a despised tax collector, has to climb a tree to see Jesus. Jesus picks Zacchaeus out of the crowd and asks if he will put him up for the night. That's straight out of a TV sitcom. I also love the reply that Paul gives to Agrippa when he is chained before him having just given his testimony. Agrippa says, 'You almost persuade me to become a Christian.' Paul replies, 'I would to God that not only you, but also all who hear me today, might become such as I am – except for these chains.' Wonderful, that must have made them laugh, 'except for these chains'.

If the New Testament has some funny stuff in it the Old Testament is full of it; the exploits of Jonah for example would make a great comedy movie. Satire is a popular method to deal with issues in the Old Testament like idolatry, as in the witty put-down of Isaiah (see Is. 44:9–20), which seems to have a very tongue in cheek description of an idolater's idiotic routine: 'Half of it [a tree trunk] he burns in the fire. Over the half he eats meat, he roasts it and is satisfied. Also he warms himself and says, "Aha, I am warm, I have seen the fire!" And the rest of it he makes into a god, his idol, and falls down to it and worships it. He prays to it and says, "Deliver me, for thou art my god!"' (Is. 44:16,17, esv). There is yet more glee when Elijah challenges the prophets of Baal on Mount Carmel. He really is 'taking the Michael' here: 'Cry aloud, for he is a god. Either he is musing, or he is relieving himself, or he is on a journey, or perhaps he is asleep and must be awakened.' (1 Kgs. 18:27, ESV). Actually, regardless of the individual incidents, the message of the Bible on a very simple level is a transformation from unhappiness to happiness: the very goal of a comedian! 'Blessed are you that weep now, for you shall laugh' (Lk. 6:21, ESV).

Of course we don't need to look to the Bible to know that God has a sense of humour, well actually we do in a way because the Bible tells us that we are made in his image, which includes our attributes of love, anger, jealousy, joy, etc. If we are made in his image we just have to look at ourselves, the human race, to see that we have a sense of humour, so he must, too. Simple really.

How should Christians use comedy?

I don't think any sensible Christian would argue against the idea that comedy is both good and godly, but it's good to know why. The type of comedy each Christian would accept, however, varies a whole lot. In fact, the amount of comedy Christians will accept varies, too. Good preachers are funny but if they are too funny, well, some Christians just start to doubt their spirituality. I know preachers who have had this problem. But why? We don't question a preacher's spirituality if they are too kind, too patient or too loving, do we? But if a preacher is just gifted with a great sense of humour, he or she has too much joy, then maybe 'they're not that spiritual'. I don't get it!

Most Christians like comedy in the church environment but get nervous when it's just comedy for comedy's sake. If there isn't a reason then some see it as flippant, but it's part of God's character, it has as much right to be there as anger, love or sorrow. One thing I am very thankful for is that I am part of a church that laughs a lot.

Of course, the big question in all of this debate is: what is OK for me to laugh at as a Christian? Does God have a puritanical comedy taste? The answer to this of course is very subjective. Does his taste follow a sort of childish conservatism or does it have an edge? Does God laugh at people and situations? It's an interesting thought: comedy by its nature very often (though not always) has a victim, even if that victim is imaginary. What I may think is a suitable joke to laugh at may very well be seen as extremely ungodly by the person in the next seat or stackable plastic chair ... and I don't intend to start writing out some guidelines. I do, however, think that God laughs at us – just as a father laughs at his children as he watches them play and do silly things or make mistakes, but if we fall he grabs us and picks us up. It's not a nasty or vindictive laughter. It couldn't be – he is God and that is not in his nature. It's a fatherly loving laughter.

Can we laugh at each other? Can we tease and make fun of each other? I think we can. I think it's one of the joys of life that we don't take each other too seriously at times. I do it for a living. Those who have seen my shows know that I poke fun at members of my audience quite vigorously. Comedy, however, is a very powerful tool and it can easily hurt or offend either intentionally or accidentally. I make a point of watching my 'audience victims' very carefully to make sure they are happy with what I am saying and doing but it is a fine line. Thankfully, 99.9 per cent of the time I don't have a problem but there have been two or three occasions in the last ten years when I have had a few hiccoughs. I was once totally misunderstood by a guy in the front row of the audience at a Christian comedy event. He was smiling and laughing with me as I teased him about this and that when suddenly I noticed the smile fade from his face. I immediately dropped my interaction with him and moved on with my routine and spoke to others. At the end of the show he came up to me and was very angry that I had made fun of his stutter. I didn't even know he had a stutter and even if I did I would never use that information for laughs. I must have stumbled over some word or other and he thought I was making fun of him.

Sometimes it is other people who get upset on another person's behalf (and usually wrongly). I once did a show at a large Christian festival where there was a lady who was about 70 years old sat among a group of much younger people in the front row of the audience. I began to chat to her and made jokes about her being older than the rest: 'Would you like some cocoa? Don't policemen look young these days?' etc. She was laughing heartily throughout and was obviously happy with the treatment. At the end of the show, as the audience were leaving, the arts coordinator for the festival came up to me and expressed concern that I had been making fun of the old lady. As he was talking to me, the old lady in question came up to us and interrupted the conversation, 'Excuse me,' she said, 'can I just say thank you very much for giving me so much fun. My husband died six months ago and this is the first time I have been able to laugh since he was alive.' Needless to say, the arts coordinator shut up.

Doing comedy and making people laugh is a risky business and you may come across some helpful Christian 'brothers and sisters' who ask you 'How dare you teach that?!', 'How dare you wear that?!' or 'How dare you say that?!'. And sometimes it's good to think about the questions because they may be valid. But Jesus went up against people like this a lot. And we know he called some of them Pharisees, actually it was more like whitewashed tombs with dry bones inside ... Nice image. So don't let them get to you.

If you stay close to God, he will make it clear to you if things aren't right about what you are doing or saying. I have dropped things and changed things in my act because God has prodded me about them.

So in answer to the question: 'does and should Christian comedy exist?' the answer is a resounding yes. In fact, I would go so far as to say that laughter and comedy *are* Christian – our God invented them. Comedy and laughter are part of who our God is. Just like Larry Norman wrote, 'Why should the devil have all the good music?' I'd like to echo that with 'Why should the devil have all the good comedy?' So don't avoid being funny because you are afraid of making mistakes, or you think you will be seen as less 'reverent'. Revel in it, and if you get the humour wrong, someone gets upset or you think you've overstepped the mark, do what you should do with so many things on this jolly Christian walk of life, say sorry, get forgiven, brush yourself down and try again … I do it all the time!

www.john-archer.com

Humour is just another defence against the universe.

(Mel Brooks)

6

Ferris Bueller's Day Off

LEE JACKSON

I was on holiday with my family and my mam and dad on the west coast of Ireland. It is never very hot in August but a great experience!

We had been there for a few days, on the beach with the kids and staying in an old cottage, and then, obviously, it was really important that we all got a bit of time to ourselves. So I signed up for a surf lesson! Now any of my friends reading this are probably laughing out loud at this shock revelation. It is not a pretty sight imagining this 35-year-old man in a dodgy hired wetsuit, but hey, I thought go for it, so I did. I paid my money and went along at 10 a.m. in the morning for my first ever surf lesson and the wetsuit was certainly needed – it was freezing cold in August! We did a few warm ups on the beach and learnt the basic skills, and then the big moment: we went out there in the sea, about 20 of us ranging from 8-year-old girls right through to one guy who was even older than me(!). (We were both really embarrassed about the whole wetsuit thing; it was a comedy classic trying to get into it!)

We waded out, the waves were massive and we had to fight just to walk out and then you do the whole 'drift along the beach and you don't realise' thing that you have to fight your way back up the beach again. It was a major fight against the waves just to get a quick go on the surfboard. I almost got to my feet at one point but ended up in the sea face down most of the time. We did this for a couple of hours until we were worn out. Clare came to meet me on the beach after the lesson – she'd gone for a coffee and walked along the beach to meet me. She said that she could see my smile from hundreds of yards down the beach and could tell that it had been an amazing experience for me.

Decision

It was like I had to make a decision there and then in my lesson: 'Am I going to enjoy this? Or am I going to be miserable?' Being an adopted Yorkshireman, because I'd paid the money, I was going to enjoy it! And the freedom of the waves, the battling, the fighting, the fun – it was an amazing experience and I will never forget it. I'm not going to be a pro-surfer any time soon, but I did enjoy the day!

As I came away and thought about the whole experience, I realised that I wanted to write a chapter around this issue ... How do we make the most of the day-to-day stuff? How do we make the most of something which could be boring, difficult, something which could be potentially embarrassing? I learnt that day that we need to get out a bit more, get out of our comfort zone, learn new skills, make the most of our opportunities. Like I didn't do once ... Clare said I couldn't write this book unless I told you the following story, ahem. A while back, I went to a Christmas ball with Clare and my friends, Justin and Esti, and we had a good meal and a talk but then the disco revved up. Now, I am a DJ and have spent loads of my life encouraging people to get into the music but I am not a dancer myself, unless bad break-dancing counts. I've been asked by Clare and others to dance loads of times but I had got it into my head that I wasn't going to and went into myself – I've been asked if I was OK on more than occasion. But it was not until a few days afterwards that it all came out – because I hadn't danced I had really upset Clare and she was annoyed that I had been so miserable (and to be fair I was). Even though I am mortally embarrassed about dancing, ten minutes on the dance floor wouldn't have killed me! And I had been feeling sorry for myself and couldn't get my head out of my bum long enough to realise that Clare really needed me to dance with her. We may go this year – Clare is in counselling about it now, only another 456 sessions to go!

One of the greatest lies that I think is told to men, or always implied to men, is that the grass is always greener somewhere else. In other words, 'If only I could do that then life would be better', 'If I was somewhere else right now life would be better', 'If I could only get that promotion then my life would be much better', 'If my girlfriend would only be like ... then life would be so much better', 'If my church was more like this, life would be so much better.' It is this lie which becomes almost part of us, that we always want to be somewhere else. When I was in the Irish Sea with the waves thrashing down on me, this portly figure in his forty-seventh-hand wetsuit (I dread to think how much wee was in it), I had to decide that I was going to enjoy the moment there and then or coast through it wishing I was somewhere else. There is an important lesson for us here: in life we have to decide to make the most of the moment we are in.

Bad

Billy Connolly once said, 'There is no such thing as bad weather, there is only inappropriate clothing' and I think

I am definitely with Billy on that one. He speaks a lot of sense. Yes, we go on holiday and it's not perfect and maybe we haven't got as much money as we want to spend and maybe it's too hot, maybe it's too cold, but actually we have the ability to make the most of what we've got. We have a decision to make almost every minute of the day. My friend Andy Lenton taught me that. He is so positive it almost makes you vomit.

Being from the north-east of England, we don't have many home-grown stars so we usually keep a close eye on people in the media who are from our area. My favourite TV programme is probably *Auf Wiedersehen Pet* starring Jimmy Nail, Tim Healy and Kevin Whateley, but two other northerners who I really respect are Ant and Dec. No, really!! Ant and Dec started off on the kids' TV show *Biker Grove*, as PJ and Duncan they developed their careers after that show into making two or three really bad records, one of them now has become a cheese-tastic classic. What you get from them when you see them,[1] is a sense of fun. These young Geordie lads from a dodgy kids' programme, who aren't particularly talented, are suddenly making the most of everything they've got. They said, 'We have had our ups and downs so we have really appreciated the good times. We have a lot of fun and we love going to work and it's as simple as that.' Ant and Dec only live a few doors away from each other in London, they spend time hanging out and working with each other. They seem to have grasped something that I think a lot of Christian men just miss the point of, and that is they seem to get the most from their day, and they seem to get the most from their work. Both of them just turning 30, they have learnt this important lesson that you appreciate the good times because there will be bad times as well. They got a lot of hassle about their PJ and Duncan characters and their hit singles, and they have had TV shows rejected, enormous criticism from the press for being popular, but they just seem to take it on board and decide to make the most of what they have got. They don't fit any media stereotypes, they are just friends presenting family TV. It defies logic, there is no funny or straight man and they can't tap dance!

> For myself I am an optimist – it does not seem to be much use being anything else.
>
> (Sir Winston Churchill)

Security

Steve is a good friend. He started a journey into the unknown and I mean literally a journey into the unknown. Steve prayer walks parts of the UK and Europe. He has recently started a new prayer walk. God has told him not to finish it yet, so he has just kept on walking. He has followed the finger of God, and in these days of careers and financial security that is such a radical thing to do. It's a real journey, literally taking every day as it comes. Asking, 'What does God want from me today? What is the Spirit saying to me?' and taking every little step in faith.

> People I know who are, by and large, happy, are the ones who are doing what they enjoy doing.
>
> (Douglas Coupland, interviewed on www.Damaris.org)

So often we wish we were somewhere else with different people, different responsibilities, or, the 'no-responsibilities' 'I'll get a motorbike' classic mid-life crisis stuff! But people like Steve are literally 'walking into the unknown', following God's prompting with no regular appointments or salary. An amazing bloke, who will be really embarrassed that I am writing about him.

The idea behind following God is that we don't wish we were somewhere else or think that we have no choice, rather that we simply follow him on a daily basis. It's almost as if we have to 'suck the life out of that day' so we can see what God will do through us. The one thing we have the most control over is our attitude; as Charles R. Swindoll said, life is 10 per cent what happens to you and 90 per cent how you react to it.

> I would say to the House, as I said to those who have joined this government: 'I have nothing to offer but blood, toil, tears, and sweat.'
>
> (Sir Winston Churchill)

Sometimes I think that's exactly what we have got to do, perhaps how it's meant to be. Sometimes even when you are in a position which is difficult, a position where you think that God might have left you, a position where you think 'this could be so much better', you can still offer everything that you have to make that situation turn around. Sometimes I think the church has over-spiritualised 'guidance' and created over-dependence on God. I think life is just about knowing who you are and getting on with it! I do wonder how the early church got on under the harsh conditions they experienced, where they put their lives on the line every day and just got on with what they knew was right.

When asked what he thought of LIVE 8, political pundit Andrew Marr replied, 'There are no movements only moments, we must decide what to do with each moment.'[2] It is so easy to criticise and be negative, it's easy to be a passenger in life, maybe we just need to get off our backsides and take advantage of the moments given to us. Psychologists say that men can be physically or emotionally absent, not wanting to engage with the world around us. Sad.

> It's a beautiful day, don't let it slip away.
>
> (U2, 'Beautiful Day')

The second most quoted verse in the Bible is probably Jn. 10:10. In *The Message* it says, 'I came so they can have real and eternal life, more and better life than they ever dreamed of.' When you hear something as often as that it becomes very familiar to you but let's put that verse into context. In the first part of the verse, Jesus says, 'A thief is only there to steal and kill and destroy.' I think often for us men there are things that can destroy us, they can steal life from us, making us want to be somewhere else instead of making the most of that particular moment. Sometimes that means action, sometimes of course it means learning to sit still – something we find harder to do these days.

> Life moves pretty fast. If you don't stop and look around once in a while you could miss it.
>
> (From the eighties classic, John Hughes' film
> *Ferris Bueller's Day Off*, Paramount Pictures, 1986)

The out-laws

To be honest though, this is a struggle for me and for many blokes. When I go to family functions, church events, and other men's activities you see so many men who are passengers, you can see it in their faces and body language.

They want to be somewhere else. I have been in many situations myself where I have had to take advantage there and then, otherwise it would be a complete waste of my time and God's.

Selwyn Hughes, in his book *Why Revival Waits* (CWR, 2003), says, 'When I was a student of theology I learnt this: there are two rails laid down in scripture – one is God's sovereignty and the other is human responsibility. If you do away with human responsibility you have nothing to save; if you do away with God's sovereignty you have nothing to save with.'

The Bible will not make sense to you unless you are prepared to run on both those rails. In the context of talking about revivals that have happened, Selwyn Hughes says that part of it is down to God and part of it is down to us. We have to pray that God puts us in situations where we can be of use, but it is still down to us to make the most of those chances. His primary tools on earth are you and me; I don't think he has a plan B!

> Yesterday is gone, tomorrow has not come, we only have today, let us begin.
>
> (Mother Teresa)

For discussion

Make the most of these!

- Think about then share a grumpy moment you have had!

- Why does God want to use us and not do it all for us?

- 'God doesn't require us to succeed; he only requires that you try.' (Mother Teresa). Discuss.

- Be accountable now, and share a situation that you need to 'step up in' the next time you face it.

- How do horoscopes, tarot cards, etc. and pre-destination (ooh, big word!) affect people's attitudes to daily life?

- Pray.

Notes

[1] In the UK, Ant and Dec have presented *I'm a Celebrity Get Me Out of Here, Pop Idol, Saturday Night Takeaway* and many other programmes.

[2] During the BBC broadcast of the concert.

Wise men make more opportunities than they find.

(Francis Bacon)

7

Calvin Smith

BAZ GASCOYNE

Athletics has been something I have been interested in from an early age. I used to love running at school. I would frequently dream about running in the 100 metres and 200 metres Olympic final for my country as I ran down the cobble alley to my grandparents' house.

Names like Jessie Owens, Don Quarrie, Valerie Bortzov, Alan Wells, Linford Christie, Carl Lewis, Ben Johnson, Calvin Smith, Donovan Bailey, Maurice Green, Dennis Mitchell, Dwain Chambers and Asafa Powell have all brought me immense pleasure and frustration over the years as I have watched them trying to become the fastest man in the world in their era. One man above any other sprinter has had a huge impact over my life in the last couple of years. That man is Calvin Smith.

I, like many other people, receive forests of mail advertising the next conference or event I should attend to help me become a better person! Every year, the same thing would happen: publicity would land on the mat and I would read it. Easter People, Spring Harvest, Soul Survivor, Keswick, Grapevine, Harvest, New Frontiers, Pioneer, Salt and Light, Cliff College, Kingdom Faith – the list goes on and on and on. (I do need to mention that I believe conferences to be good and I have benefited immensely from them in my walk with God and my work.) Each year I would read the publicity and then get frustrated and angry. I would look at the list and photos of all the speakers and think, 'Why not me?' I know that's so arrogant, and perhaps none of you have ever felt like that and never will, but I did. I would look and think, 'Well OK, he's not a bad speaker but I could do just as good as him or better.' And I would make a judgement on whether they were still 'doing the stuff' in the real world, or had become professional Christian conference speakers. And I would grade them one to ten on the 'Baz Gascoyne Speaking Quality Monitor'. Am I the only person who has hoped for a flu epidemic over the people speaking (or leading worship, or prophesying, or praying) so the phone would ring with a request for *my* gifting?

One day I was talking to God about this, asking him why I was so insecure and desperate to have my name in a glossy brochure. I remember Jeff Lucas once saying that God had brought him down to size once after speaking really well by saying something like, 'Way to go, Jeff – famous for 15 minutes at Spring Harvest, you have really made it!' After whingeing, shouting and moaning at God, and not getting a response, I eventually shut my big mouth to pause for breath and this thought entered my mind: 'Ben Johnson.' What the hell was I thinking about an athlete for when I was having a go at God for not getting me a speaking gig at a national event? 'Ben Johnson'. Was it the cheese from lunchtime or could it actually be God speaking to me? 'Ben Johnson.' What does God know about athletics? I know I was pushing it a bit now so said, 'OK God, you have my attention. What are you saying to me?'

I knew Ben Johnson was famous for breaking the world record in 1987 and winning the most famous Olympic 100 metres ever run, back in 1988 in Seoul. I also knew that two days later he was disqualified for failing a drug test.

The media at the time reported that he had his medal taken off him and the world record removed from the records.

'Is that it, God?' I asked.

'No.'

'Well, what then?'

Then God asked me a question that was going to change my whole way of thinking: 'Who came fourth?'

'Say what, God?'

'Who came fourth?'

I had no idea. I knew Carl Lewis had come second and Linford Christie third but I had no idea who came fourth. With Johnson being disqualified it meant Lewis had become the winner, Christie had moved up to silver and the well-known athlete whose name I couldn't remember came third. No matter how much I tried to remember his name or picture his face I could not. Fourth place to bronze, but this still did not help me identify his name, even though I must have seen the race at least 50 times since the event.

At a time like this the only thing to do is turn to your loyal and trusted friend www.google.co.uk. There were over 200,000 pages about Ben Johnson. As I began to read about that most famous race which took place on 27 September 1988, I discovered the name of the mystery athlete who moved from fourth to third place. Moreover, I finally discovered the huge lesson that God wanted to teach me.

Calvin Smith was the name of the mystery athlete and as I read more about that race and the athletes who took part, God's message to me was clear: 'Baz, all I want you to be is a Calvin Smith.' I knew Calvin Smith had been a good runner and learnt that he had been a double world 200 metres champion and in 1983 had set a new world record at Colorado Springs for the 100 metres at 9.93 seconds, breaking the previous record which had

stood for 15 years. But what did God mean? As I continued
to read the information on the web page, a lesson began to
unfold that I want to not only talk about but live.

What I love about God is how he gets your attention
through something you are interested in or have some
knowledge about, then once he has your attention begins
to reveal what he wants to say. This is what he did
often through the prophets and Jesus, using every day
things to bring some revelation, correction, direction or
encouragement, knowing he had the people's attention.

What did I learn from Calvin Smith? Well, most people,
including myself initially, had no idea who had come
fourth and then moved up to third place in probably the
most famous 100 metres Olympic final ever. 'Baz, he may
not have come first in the world arena, but he did finish
and he did well and this is what I am wanting for you. It's
not about having your picture in some glossy magazine,
but it is about being faithful right to the end.'

We read in Heb. 12:1–2 (NIV):

> Therefore, since we are surrounded by such a great
> cloud of witnesses, let us throw off everything that
> hinders and the sin that so easily entangles, and let
> us run with perseverance the race marked out for us.
> Let us fix our eyes on Jesus, the author and perfecter
> of our faith, who for the joy set before him endured
> the cross, scorning its shame, and sat down at the
> right hand of the throne of God.

So I began to thank God for speaking to me and challenging
my motives, and asked him to help me be a Calvin Smith:
someone who will do their best and finish no matter what
I am asked to do.

But there was more, and as I continued to read some
of the articles, nothing could have prepared me for what I

was going to read and what God was seeking to impress on my mind. Below is a section of an article that I read:

> When Calvin Smith came to the line for the 100 metres final in Seoul, he was a double world 200 metres champion and he had held the 100 metres world record. He knew what it was like to be the fastest man in the world, but he was also aware that there was no longer a level playing field on which to prove it:
>
> 'Throughout the last five or ten years of my career, I knew I was being denied the chance to show that I was the best clean runner,' he says. 'Our governing body was letting athletes run who I knew were not clean. Everyone knew drugs were a problem, but nothing was being done about it. It was as if drugs were OK, as long as you didn't go over the top.
>
> 'From running against runners week after week, you know what athletes are capable of, you know their physique and you can sometimes see it in their eyes. There are signs that something is different. But what can you do?' In that 100 metres in Seoul, Smith could do nothing. 'I'd worked so hard because I knew I was competing against athletes who were on drugs,' he recalls. 'I was at a disadvantage. Drugs were a problem and the problem was not being handled by the IAAF. That was discouraging. I was in very good condition.'
>
> (*The Athlete Calvin Smith*, by Owen Slot, 24 September 2003, www.timesonline.co.uk/ article/0,,9080-828226,00.html)

Now that I was reading articles claiming that Ben Johnson wasn't the only runner in that race who may have taken drugs my attention was held.

Smith goes on to say:

> ... There was another athlete who tested positive
> (Linford Christie) and something should have been
> done about him, but, again, they didn't want to
> tarnish the Games.

Owen Slot continued:

> ... if you take Johnson and Christie out of the
> picture, there was only Carl Lewis ahead of Smith in
> that final and Smith is keenly aware that Lewis has
> been embroiled in a recent drugs controversy.

What I was reading was amazing: it was not just Johnson
but Lewis and Christie who also were being tarnished with
reports of drugs, suggesting they, too, should have been
disqualified and banned. In an *Observer/Guardian* article,
the following read:

> Lewis failed three tests at the 1988 Olympic trials
> (these were covered up at the time) and the American
> Olympic body accepted his appeal that he had
> innocently taken a herbal supplement. Following
> the final, Christie failed a drug test for the stimulant
> ephedrine, but was later cleared on appeal after
> convincing the panel he had taken it inadvertently
> when drinking ginseng tea. The 1992 Olympic gold
> medallist then received a two year ban in 1999 after
> testing positive for nandrolone.

In this article, entitled 'The most corrupt race ever', Ben
Johnson is quoted as saying:

> Yes, I was taking steroids, but so were others on the
> starting line that day. They know it. I know it. That's
> all that counts. If people are naïve enough to believe
> that athletes don't take drugs, that is their problem.

> (http://observer.guardian.co.uk/osm/story/
> 0,6903,1270863,00.html)

Was this someone who had been found out just trying to make what he did more acceptable or could it be true? As I continued reading this article, it claimed that five out of the eight who ran have since failed drug tests.

If you go on to http://images.thetimes.co.uk/TGD/picture/0,,89015,00.jpg dated 12/06/2004, you will see a great photo of the finish of the race with details of each athlete and the substances they may have been taking.

Whatever the truth or otherwise of these articles, I wanted to know what God was trying to say to me. As I quietly pondered on what these articles were implying, I felt God was saying, 'Baz, the most important thing is that you keep your life clean. Keep short accounts with me and others.'

As the writer of the book of Hebrews said 'throw off everything that hinders'. Insecurities and jealousy were certainly hindering my walk with God at this time and I needed to throw them off and let my security be in God and not in performance.

Questions

'Let us throw off everything that hinders and the sin that so easily entangles.'

- What sin is currently entangling you?
- What things are hindering you from running the race?
- What is the race that God has set out before you and wants you to run?
- Is there anything that you started and then put down before you'd finished? Is God asking you to pick it up again?

On a man's road trip, the strongest bladder determines pit stops not the weakest.

8

A Life That Counts!

STEVE LOWTON

As I write, it is exactly one year to the day that my wife and I found ourselves in a city called Hefei, right in the heart of China. We had just spent an amazing weekend in Shanghai, the Hong Kong of that great nation, but now, after a five-hour train ride and three years of soul searching and form filling, we found ourselves being ushered into a hotel room to be given our 9-month-old baby girl. Kathy and I were here at the invitation of the Chinese authorities and because of our decision to adopt one of the many orphaned children that brings shame upon the world in which we live.

This is not the place to go into all the issues of adoption and the incredible need for mums and dads across the world. Indeed, I would say that there are many others far more qualified than I am to write on this subject. I know of one couple, for instance, who have chosen not to have their own children. Instead, they have now adopted three, all from the same mother, who would undoubtedly have been separated from each other, spending their childhood in and out of children's homes, had they not been adopted in this way. How cool is that? Most of us will know of others who have opened their homes to foster and have done so for many years. I, however, want to write about the choices we all face to give ourselves a 'second time round'. Anyone can give himself or herself once to all that life offers. First time round, there is all the enthusiasm and excitement of the new. However, I find that I meet many men who hit the mid-forties and have run out of steam. Perhaps in their early years, much had been risked but now the most that is hoped for is an improvement to the golf handicap! To be full of passion, even into our latter years, and to be willing and able to rise above the disappointments, giving ourselves a second or third time, that's what really inspires me. It is these issues that I want to address and had to wrestle with during the three years that passed from our initial enquiries about adoption to actually getting on the plane to China. Let me explain.

Kathy and I already have two wonderful daughters. Hannah is 22 and starting a career as a psychologist, Laura is 21 and is a student on an acting course. For those of you who are parents, you will know something of the legitimate hopes carried for your kids. There is the wonder of seeing some of these fulfilled, coupled with the disappointments and heartache that life inevitably throws up. For us, as followers of Jesus, and two people who had given the best part of our lives to growing and planting a church, it has been very painful to see both our daughters seemingly turn their backs on Jesus and make other choices. My disappointment was in no way in my two girls. To the contrary, I am intensely proud of them both. Their love of life is wonderful to see and their dislike of all that is religious and hollow, totally understandable. No, my disappointment was with myself and, if I am honest, with the God to whom I had given my life. As someone who has spent many hours on the motorways, encouraging the people of God in the faith, I often felt like Abraham going to pray for the barren wombs of the household of Abimelech (see Gen. 20:17), but going painfully aware of the barrenness of his wife Sarah's womb. The result was that I carried many questions as to the nature of life, God's part in it all, and the individual choices we all face. On top of this, the ridicule I felt was imaginary and of my own making, but nevertheless profound. How could I go through a second time the whole mix of emotions that parenthood brings, choosing to rise above the self-doubt that such issues provoke? For, make no mistake about it, with our two oldest daughters beginning to make their own way in life we were, in reality, starting another family.

There was also the challenge of finance. Being itinerant in ministry does not offer the greatest job security, and having given myself to 'church work' for the last 20 years, I didn't have too many other strings to my bow! Coupled to this, with both Kathy and I in our late forties with little or no pensions, we were going to need to be earning right the way through into our late sixties and early seventies! 'Are you mad?' was often the unspoken question that many asked of us. To be fair, it was a question that we often asked of ourselves, and led me many times to leave my bed in the middle of the night to look for answers from the God of Heaven and Earth. On one such occasion, the Lord led me to the Psalms and to my favourite biblical character, David. All through my life I have loved and so identified with this passionate man. Never frightened of his own emotions, everything is laid out in the records of Scripture for us as men to learn from. Terrible weakness but also incredible strength is displayed over every twist and turn of David's pursuit of God and of life. The Psalms so encapsulate that, and so it was that I found myself meditating on Ps. 37:25: 'I was young and now I am old, yet I have never seen the righteous forsaken or their children begging bread.' It was at that moment that I knew I had a promise from God that I could lay hold of and declare out in the challenges that lay ahead. I knew that if God never spoke to me again, that I could live off that one verse for as long as there is the breath of life within me.

Lastly, there was the challenge of my marriage. Kathy and I have been, for the most part, happily married for 20 years, but with both of our daughters leaving home there were all the questions that most married couples face at such a time. Was I able to commit to another 20 years of marriage or was now a good time to think the unthinkable?! Sorry, if I offend anyone. I believe totally in the sanctity of Christian marriage and love Kathy very much. Sometimes, though, sanctity and the assumption of 'til death do us part' can become the excuse for indifference and laziness. Being willing to face the unthinkable actually gives value to our choices and the covenant that has been made. However, all that aside, let's get real. Which of us haven't thought that the grass might be greener on the other side? Starting a second family was making a pretty clear statement that I was choosing not to look.

At the same time as I was wrestling with all these questions, I was also aware of something that Kathy and I were wanting to express at this point in our lives. We have lived on the edge for so many of our years together and everything within us was crying out against the stereotype of life that called us to draw back as we got older and to settle for the safe and easy option. I hate safe and easy! Of course, the desire to feel safe is totally legitimate, and the provision of that a requirement of good fathering ... but only to permission and encourage the discovery of new adventures, and therefore all the risk that goes with that particular package. We couldn't settle for two holidays a year, comfortable bank balances and the hope of a visit from the grandchildren. There is nothing wrong with that, but we carried the conviction that all of us are capable of so much more. To us there is nothing more exciting than to see someone in their twilight years still with a wonderful love of life and taste for adventure. One such couple I know chose a few years ago to leave the leafy suburbs of Leeds and move onto one of the roughest estates within the city. Opening their home up to the kids of their street, they loved them with all the wealth of love that only those who have seen a bit of life are capable of doing. Out of their example, a children's work was birthed that later gave rise to a city-wide initiative that now sees over a thousand children visited weekly. Each of these kids now know, at least once a week, that they are going to be loved with the uniqueness that every child needs. Sadly, the life of one half of this amazing couple was tragically snatched from them through an appalling cancer. But what a legacy to leave! A whole lot better than a neat and tidy house filled with nothing more than memories, the occasional game of golf, and net curtains!

It was that sort of example that called us further down the road of adoption and our little adventure. Yes, sleepless nights would be part of the package, and the hassle of finding babysitters a reality check for us, but to follow the wild finger of God and to become afresh 'prisoners of hope' was far more exciting than any package holiday ever could be, however exotic the location!

Here I sit then, one year on from our incredible journey to China, hearing the sounds of Zhen at play and the infectious laughter that so often now fills our home. So far there is food on the table and whilst sleepless nights are many, the day always arrives! Kathy and I can look back on one of the most amazing years of our lives where we have seen the favour of God not just over us and Zhen but also over our two other wonderful daughters. Hannah is now walking with Jesus and Laura is on a journey to faith. In addition, we have a friend from Japan living with us called Miki, making it a truly international household!

Zhen's full name is Zhen Chun, a name given to her from within the orphanage. It means Spring Treasure, or new beginnings. Whether it is the meaning of her name, or the view out of the front window of the home we have these last few months moved into, I am continually reminded that the God we follow is the God of new beginnings. We live at what used to be the eastern gate of the city of Leeds; the place where the trams would turn round. Just recently a friend helped me to see the obvious, that a terminus is a place where journeys end and journeys begin. We have begun a fresh journey, imprisoned by hope and more passionate about life and love and Jesus than we have ever been. As we post off our application to explore again the possibility of going back to China to adopt a second child, I simply want to bear witness to the God who, as Scripture testifies, has given himself time and time again throughout the course of history.

Adopting a child may be your worst nightmare. That is not the issue. The issue is rather what are we living for and what will be our legacy? To help you deal with these questions, I have a few more:

- What used to make you angry or excited? Does it still? If not why not and what can you do to get in touch with the old you? Are there any of your mates who can help you in this?
- How do you want your life to count? What is stopping that from happening?
- What do you need to be willing to risk? The old business saying is that we need to speculate to accumulate. Put another way, what are you willing to speculate?
- If everything went pear-shaped, could you live with the worst case scenario? If so, what more is there to

say? It's a well-worn phrase, but if you want to see something you've never seen before, you have to do something you have never done before!

I say stuff the safe and secure. Forget about the well-trodden paths that are predictable and clear cut. Shake free of the shadows of yesterday. There's always grace to go a second time.

> As for you also, because of the blood of my covenant with you, I will set your prisoners free from the waterless pit. Return to your stronghold, O prisoners of hope; today I declare that I will return to you double.
>
> (Zech. 9:11,12, ESV)

[This chapter was originally written in early 2003. Now, three years on, Kathy and Steve are about to travel back out to China to adopt a sister for Zhen.]

There's a lot of pain, but a lot more healing.
There's a lot of trouble, but a lot more peace.
There's a lot of hate, but a lot more loving.
There's a lot of sin, but a lot more grace!

Oh Outrageous Grace! Oh Outrageous Grace!
   Love unfurled by heaven's hand.
Oh Outrageous Grace! Oh Outrageous Grace!
   Through my Jesus I can stand.

There's a lot of fear, but a lot more freedom.
There's a lot of darkness, but a lot more light.
There's a lot of cloud, but a lot more vision.
There's a lot of perishing, but a lot more Life!

Oh Outrageous Grace! Oh Outrageous Grace!
   Love unfurled by heaven's hand.
Oh Outrageous Grace! Oh Outrageous Grace!
   Through my Jesus I can stand.

There's an enemy,
That seeks to kill what it can't control.
It twists and turns,
Making mountains out of molehills.
But I will call on the Lord
Who is worthy of praise.
I run to him, and I am saved!...

By Outrageous Grace ....

(Godfrey Birtill © 2000, Thankyou Music,
used by permission. www.godfreyb.com)

9

I Need Someone With Skin On

LEE JACKSON

Shock

Sir Bob Geldof has been voted the top dad![1] It took me a while to take this in! The hero of LIVE 8 / Aid, who had two great songs that he couldn't sing very well. A super dad? A foul-mouthed scruffy man has been voted top dad in the Mothers' Union survey. Wow. What happened to all the other famous dads? I guess Beckham may have fallen from grace then?

To be honest I have actually got nothing against Sir Bob, in fact he is one of my heroes. Band Aid and Live Aid were life-changing events for me, somehow engaging the idea that music, comedy and justice can go together. But I certainly didn't have him pegged down as a top dad, yet that is what the survey says.

Sir Bob's story is harrowing. His wife, Paula Yates, former presenter of the cutting-edge music show *The Tube*, left Geldof for Michael Hutchence, singer with INXS, whom she met when interviewing him on *The Big Breakfast*, the show produced by Geldof's production company. Yates had a daughter (named Heavenly Hiraani Tigerlily) with Hutchence. When Hutchence was found dead in a hotel room in 1997, Geldof went to court and obtained full custody of his three daughters. His experiences at the time of his divorce have led him to become an outspoken advocate of fathers' rights. After Yates' death from an overdose, Geldof became the legal guardian of Tigerlily, believing that she should be raised with her three half-sisters.[2]

He took into his home, as if she was his own child, the daughter from a marriage break-up that hurt him deeply, as a sign of forgiveness and sacrifice?

As I watched LIVE 8 a few months ago, I saw that his daughters had come along to the concert and one of them was wearing an old Boomtown Rats T-shirt, as a sign of respect to their dad. It was great to see the 'Scary Irishman' in a new light.

It seems such a long time ago since writing the original chapter in *Dead Men Walking* about the birth of my twins Rhea and Lauren (maybe time does fly like my dad said it would – d'oh!). Back then we were in the hospital waiting for them to get stronger so that we could go home – that was seven years ago! They are now in their third year of schooling and are amazing little people. It is right to say that being a dad is a rollercoaster ride, as Steve Martin's character realises in the film *Parenthood*. Yet in seven years I feel I haven't learnt that much apart from how to tie back hair and make dinky packed lunches.

Researchers keep saying how important dads are in a child's life. My friend Jon and I both have two daughters and we often talk to each other about how great it is. It makes you feel special. A dad and two daughters – I wouldn't change it, though occasionally we might miss the kind of 'dad and son football' thing. One of the only things that I have learnt is that Rhea and Lauren really look up to me for encouragement and reassurance. I also noticed that from a very early age, girls do stare in the mirror and look at their own bodies, their hair, and I have noticed them almost waiting for me to encourage them, to say positive things to them. I seem to spend all day telling them how much I love them, cuddling them and listening to their very complicated stories about their friends' antics at school.

> You can't understand until you experience the simple joy the first time your son points at a seagull and says 'duck'.
>
> (Russell Crowe)

In my work with young people I notice how important dads are. In one of the schools I work in there are very few dads on the scene, and you can see that it makes an enormous difference to attitudes and behaviours. Fathers bring security and boundaries and often stability to a family. You can often tell when young people haven't had stability in their backgrounds. So there is one big thing that we have to work hard at: being the best dad that we can be (contrary to some people I think being a good dad is quantity not just quality time). It is important to be around – even today I had to cancel a few diary appointments coming up in a few weeks' time because I realised that my diary was too full and I was going to be away for too many weekends in a row. Being away too much feels uncomfortable, I miss my family and I know they miss me, so I made a few cancellations and simply made sure that I am going to be around at least two weekends in four. That makes all the difference for us. Saturdays are now special times with the kids even if it is just hanging out watching *Dick and Dom in da Bungalow* together. We do have a good laugh at the bogie game and a more relaxed time on a weekend. I do work weekends but there has to be a balance for you, your partner and your kids.

I once met a bloke who was a high-flier, he was jetting all over the world and earning big bucks, but he shared quietly with me that he was tired, lonely and he really missed his family. His life was permanently out of balance.

AAARRRGH!

If you're a dad, one of the things you need to relax about is that all dads struggle. Remember, most dads don't feel they are good dads, even if they are. We are not on our own. When doing a men's weekend a couple of years ago, one of the guys asked me if I would pray with him. He started to weep as he told me he felt he was short-tempered and negative towards his kids when they wound him up and he just wanted to be a calmer dad who smiled a bit more. So we prayed that he would have more patience with his children. I could see that it took a lot of effort for him to speak to me about that. He opened up to someone about being a dad for maybe the first time. We are all thinking at some point that we are probably not doing a very good job but it is important that we are physically there – that's half the battle! Although I have seen dads who are there but have an attitude that is so withdrawn they might as well not be there.

We all have quieter times, times when we interact, times when we don't but let's try to be spontaneous! Take your kids out for a bit. Having twins, we often take them out separately and we also encourage them to do different things so that they don't get treated as one child when there are two of them. A quick decision to go to the park with your kids is very healthy, they don't need three weeks' notice; if they are up, they are ready to go!

Fight!

There has been some research recently into 'fighting fathers'[3] which claims that they breed better-adjusted children! It is great to hear that psychologists have realised it is good to interact with your kids physically, and not to wrap them up in cotton wool, to allow them to be somehow separate from you and the world. It is refreshing to see that they are encouraging us to play, fight and roll around with your kids. Physical contact is so important for children to realise that you are a friendly face not a stoic father figure.

'I'm a father not a commandant'

There are loads of 'for dads' books and the authors will be more knowledgeable than I am for sure! Look around, see what you can find, but here is a classic:

> Over the past several years, both Norm and I have observed and counselled scores of fellow strugglers, well-meaning dads who feel almost overwhelmed by their job. Many admit that they are fumbling in the juggling act of marriage, career and fatherhood, most feel trapped by their intense work schedules and accompanying pressures by a lack of practical fathering skills by a lack of good teamwork with their wives or unhealthy patterns in their own person-alities. Because of these frustrations, too many men have virtually defaulted as fathers, becoming either absentee or uninvolved in their children's day to day development. It is a modern day family tragedy.
>
> (Josh McDowell and Norman Wakefield,
> *Dad Difference*, Victor Books, 1990)

The authors go on to say that a study of 39 teenage girls who were suffering from the Anorexia Nervosa eating disorder showed that 36 of them had one common denominator: the lack of a close relationship with their fathers. Dr Almond Nikole's research found that an emotionally- or physically-absent father contributes to a child's:

1. low motivation for achievement;
2. inability to defer immediate gratification for later rewards;
3. low self esteem;
4. susceptibility to group influence and juvenile delinquency.[4]

These stats and quotes from research show us one thing: we need to try our best to be both emotionally and physically present in our families. This doesn't mean we have to be chained to the house or physically attached to our children at all times, it just means that we have to engage with them emotionally and physically, er maybe have some fun?! So many men seem to think that being a dad is one of the worst things that has ever happened to them. Sure, you have less money now and probably don't have as much sleep (I certainly didn't have a grey hair before I had kids!), but it is a privilege. Becoming a dad is the easy bit, being a dad is much more difficult and yes, feels better.

> A small boy shouted downstairs, 'I'm scared of the dark!' His father yelled back, 'Don't be scared, God is with you.' There was silence for a moment then, 'Get up here fast. I need someone with skin on!'
>
> (Rob Parsons, *The 60 Second Father*, Broadman & Holman Publishers, 1997)

It is amazing how we train for our jobs or ministries. We develop ourselves in many ways, yet often we have not thought to sit down and discuss with our friends the joys and struggles of being a dad. Why not do it with some of your friends in the next week?

No one was ever heard to say on their deathbed, 'I wish I'd spent more time at the office.'

(Rob Parsons, *The 60 Second Father*,
Broadman & Holman Publishers, 1997)

Age

And as for ageing, well, read my dad's chapter! He has recently retired but in the meantime here is my advice ...

1. You are getting older.
2. You will die.
3. You will get grey hair and/or go bald.
4. Get over it.
5. If you can't get over it talk to somebody.
6. Now get over it.

Life is about seasons. You can't change the yearly seasons yourself but you can wear the right clothes and enjoy the new season that God brings you.

Oh yeah, and for the record, get a life – 'Just for Men' hair dye always looks like you have had your hair dyed, men's wigs, men's make-up, plastic surgery, or anything else along those lines, looks stupid and is a complete waste of money. And you will also spend all day hoping that no one will mention the fact that you have a wig, like one or two evangelists I have seen!

> Grey hair is a crown of splendour; it is attained by a righteous life.
>
> (Prov. 16:31, NIV)

Some questions for the hugely keen ...

- What has been your best dad moment so far?
- What part do you have to play in a child's life if you are not a dad?

- Becoming a dad or being a dad: which is more fun? Discuss!
- What can you learn from your dad?
- Discuss the use of 'Just for Men'.

Notes

[1] http://www.eauk.org/contentmanager/content/eamc/press/mu-180604.htm Mothers' Union survey, used with kind permission.
[2] This article is licensed under the GNU Free Documentation License. It uses material from the http://en.wikipedia.org/wiki/Bob_Geldof#Relationship_with_Paula_Yates Wikipedia article 'Bob Geldof'.
[3] Research conducted by Professor Charlie Lewis from Lancaster University.
[4] Almond Nikole Jr, 'Changes in the American Family' Whitehouse paper.

My wife says I never listen to her, at least I think that's what she said ...

10

Ebenezer Scrooge

BAZ GASCOYNE

Job interviews are always an experience. They can be the most daunting thing in the world or the most exciting, depending on your personality type. Over the years, I have had various interviews but there are two that stand out in my memory. In one, I was not even aware that the interview had begun. I had just arrived in the room to face the panel of five when tea, coffee and biscuits were brought in. They helped themselves and asked me what I would like and as I drank the tea and chatted to the panel I thought we were having a tea break. Forty minutes later, I was thanked and that was that. It went great and I answered all the questions freely because I was not nervous. Two days later I was offered the job.

Another interview I recall was on the south coast in the mid-eighties. I had been asked by a church to go down and meet the minister and leaders with the possibility of becoming their youth worker. So I caught a train from Darlington and headed down to meet these people to see what the church was doing and what the job entailed. They were doing a great job among teenagers, with a thriving church youth group and a massive youth club. They had great links with the local schools, both junior and senior, and altogether had something like 250–300 young people coming through their doors weekly.

The meetings went well and I was impressed with their activities and vision. They informed me a decision would be made after a church vote, and the next day I was back on the train, excited about the prospect of working for them, and hoping the vote would go in my favour.

In the end I turned the job down, even though the vote was unanimous. Why? Because of that age-old problem in the church: money. Why is it that anything to do with money and the church is like Ebenezer Scrooge has come back to life, shouting 'Bah, Humbug!' They were going to provide accommodation for me and then pay me £15 ($27) a week. However, it had cost me over £60 ($90) for a return ticket on the train to go for the interview. Whenever I wanted to go home to visit it would cost me more than a month's salary. I would have to save two months' salary with out spending a penny to have enough for the train fare and spending money.

After speaking to my friends, I was sure I was making the right decision but, for obvious reasons, the discussion with the church was not easy. At the end of the telephone conversation, I heard those famous words, 'You are not doing it for the money, but for the love of the Lord.'

Oh how I wanted to say, 'Well *you* live on what you want to give me and I will live on what *you* receive,' but I didn't. And it's possible the minister's salary wasn't much better. God is not tight so why does the church behave like it at times?

Some of the funniest evenings I have had are drinking and laughing with a group of men, all of whom have been shafted by churches and Christians, but when I hear their stories I hope one day we will learn.

I remember one evening after a great concert in Sheffield for about 1,000 people, the band, PA guys and organisers all went out for a curry. During the evening, two of my mates stood up and made a toast to a gentleman who ran a Christian management music company, nearly causing a riot by their actions as some of the band members started swearing, shouting and even throwing food. Why? Because they said they had been cheated out of thousands of pounds owed to them.

I once spoke at a church in Sheffield where a small brown envelope with the words 'For the preacher' written on it had been placed in the pulpit. I discreetly placed it in my pocket and carried on with the service. At the end of the service I left to go home. As I walked home, the sky turned grey and the heavens opened – thunder and lightning, the works. I got drenched but decided it couldn't get any worse so carried on home. How wrong I was. After about three minutes walking, I stood in a massive load of dog poo covering not only the sole but also the laces of my shoe. How blessed I felt. This must be as bad as it gets. Oh no, the end of my trousers caught the big dollop on my shoe which rubbed itself in nicely. I eventually arrived home, wet, smelly and cold and desperate to get out of these clothes. After showering and warming up, I decided to open the envelope that was given to me by the church. How much had they decided to bless me with for the preparation, the service I had taken, plus costs incurred? I opened the envelope and a £1 coin fell out on the floor.

My friend Steve and I were asked to go and speak at a university some years ago, approximately 70 miles away. So we drove there, spoke at the event and then were invited out for a drink by some of the members of the Christian Union. On the way we were given an envelope for our services with £25 inside. I know that students don't have much money, but what happened next still brings a smile to my face. We entered the pub and approached the bar where we were asked by one of the students what we were drinking. We both replied, 'A pint of lager, please.'

All the drinks came, including the students'; the students disappeared and we were left to pay the bill of £23. On the way home we stopped and bought ourselves a Mars bar each and a bottle of water which left us £1.27. Our payment for the evening – fantastic.

Friends of mine who did a concert were given a cheque at the end of the evening which didn't cover the amount agreed at the time of the booking. When questioned, the organiser replied, 'Oh don't worry, we have got you something else, seeing as it's nearly Christmas.' He then produced a box full of 200 mince pies. That's really going to help pay the bills! I asked my mate what they did with them. His answer made me laugh and still does today: 'We threw every bloody one out at the cars on our journey home.' Merry Christmas everybody!

Another friend of mine did a whole weekend for a church and they paid him with a small amount of money, some toilet rolls and a big lump of cheese!

I heard this week that someone who was asked to work at an event in Harrogate this summer for a whole week was paid £10 in a gift voucher. I am sure this covered all their expenses, the preparation work they put in before the week and what they did during the week. I am also certain that the main speakers would not have accepted this so why should someone who maybe is not a household name in Christendom have to? I often want to ask people how they would feel if their secular bosses paid them in a similar manner.

Over 13 years ago, I was asked to speak at a youth event and a Sunday meeting for a church down in Chichester. The lesson I learnt there about being generous has never left me. Even though I spoke badly at the youth event, and only did OK on the Sunday morning, the gift I received covered all my expenses with a generous amount on top as a blessing. I certainly *was* blessed. I remember saying to my wife Linda if we ever became church leaders I would be adamant that we bless those who came and served us as a church. Well, today we are in that fortunate position and it is an ethos of our church to be generous. We learnt a key lesson from our friends at Revelation church in Chichester that we are determined to maintain.

Why do so many churches find it hard to give generously? Perhaps they have never really experienced the generosity of God themselves, not just in finances but also his love and grace.

Unfortunately, Ebenezer Scrooge is still alive and kicking in many churches and Christian organisations. We need to kill him off once and for all and demonstrate the lavish generosity of God's love and grace in all our financial dealings.

Church committees are not a vocation.

11

Mr Tinky and t'Internet

LEE JACKSON

I'm too shy to express my sexual needs except over
the phone to people I don't know.
(Garry Shandling, US comedian
and television actor)

You were all expecting it so here it is – the porn and
masturbation chapter!

The next page of the book is to test your bravery, let the
book fall open in public preferably on a train or in church
– if you dare ...

'PORN AND MASTURBATION'

That's better – lets get it out in the open!

- Nine out of ten kids aged between 8 and 16 have viewed porn online, mostly accidentally whilst doing homework.[1]
- 30 per cent of all unsolicited emails contain pornographic information.[2]
- 60 per cent of all website visits are sexual in nature.[3]
- 51 per cent of church pastors admit that looking at Internet pornography is their biggest temptation.[4]
- 37 per cent of pastors say it is a current struggle and four out of ten have visited a porn website.[5]
- Every day up to 30 million people log on to pornographic websites.[6]
- Research shows that heavy exposure to media sex is associated with an increased perception of the frequency of sexual activity in the real world, as a result, television may function as a kind of 'super peer' normalising these behaviours and thus, encouraging them among teenagers.[7]
- It is also believed that 70 per cent of women involved in pornography are survivors of incest or child sexual abuse.[8]

It is no wonder that we have to write an honest book like this, because we have to deal with life differently now. Gone are the days when in order to see porn you had to go through the embarrassment of greeting (or stealing from) the local shopkeeper who knows your mum, or maybe worse, borrowing a dodgy mag off a friend! Now most people, old and young, both in the workplace and at home, have free and easy access to Internet porn within a few seconds of switching on their computer. In fact, while I am typing this at home right now, it would only take me a few seconds on a search engine and I could be immersed in a world of porn. The world has changed, so we have to as well.

It is important to be realistic as well. Pornography isn't a fun thing which is passed around the office as videos were at my first job in a solicitors' office – it can be an extremely serious problem for a lot of men.

> Internet pornography is a ticking time bomb with a capacity to wreck countless families.
>
> (www.eauk.org)

The statistics are staggering. More than 25 per cent of the pornographic sites visited in Britain were from home PCs and in 2004 British Telecom revealed that it is blocking more than 10,000 attempts each day to access child pornography. In the Care survey of 3,000 church leaders in 2001, 97 per cent of church leaders indicated they felt that pornography was a serious problem and almost all felt that they lacked the resources to help people.

> It was estimated there were 1.3 million porn websites and the cyber sex industry generates approximately $1 billion annually. This is expected to grow to $5 to $7 billion over the next 5 years.
>
> (National Research Council report 2002 in the US)

These stats make the situation real to us. Many of you reading this will have already visited porn websites and some of you may be using Internet porn on a regular basis to masturbate. Somehow we can persuade ourselves that it is not much of a problem. We can think it is trivial.

> Internet pornography is accessible, affordable and almost anonymous and it can appear secret and safe. No Internet application is immune from pornography which is why it is so important to be careful when surfing alone.
>
> (From the article on www.Care.org.uk/anon)

It is usually a secret, not many people will know about it, apart from your wife or your girlfriend, even if you think they don't. It is a temptation for most men and for some women, and it is definitely addictive. Some men with particular addictive personalities may only need to visit a website once to be addicted for many years to come. Of course, there are many other dangers as well. As you make yourself accustomed to air-brushed false images of perfect women with almost grotesque breasts which the industry has demanded over the years, it is going to affect your relationship with your wife. How can normal women without surgery and an air-brush be expected to compete with the perfect images that men often view on a daily basis? It affects relationships, it affects families and in extreme cases can cause them to completely break down.

> Pornography is a sexual cul-de-sac. It goes nowhere worth the price paid in getting there.
>
> (*Searching for Intimacy*, Lyndon Bowring (ed), Authentic Media, 2005, used with kind permission)

> To reject pornography is to take a stand for sex as a special way of expressing and deepening interpersonal commitment.
>
> (John Hugh Court, *Pornography a Christian Critique*, InterVarsity Press, 1980)

Those who discover the joy in life from the sacred gift of sex will find the plastic substitute of porn losing its power over them. Sex is brilliant! But like anything else it can be tainted and made ungodly. A bit like a bad remix of a good song that you hear only as a low quality MP3. It sounds so bad it puts you off the real song.

Why?

So, why do people actually use porn?

Pornography can seem especially attractive to those who are:

- coping with stress and peer pressure;
- curious/exploring;
- depressed;
- fearful of intimacy;
- feeling low self-worth and believing no one will love them;
- having unsatisfactory sexual experiences – they think this will help them find stimulation or remove pressure from their spouse if used as a source of personal stimulation;
- feeling they have a high sex drive;
- lonely;
- needing help in their marriage;
- needing to escape reality;

- single and celibate, pornography can seem a better option than having a sexual relationship.

(From www.care.org.uk / anon)

What if we want to get some help? Here are a few pointers:

1. Understand that you're not alone. Many men suffer from similar addictions and many of them are happy to talk about it, and how they found their way out of it.

2. God is a more graceful God than you ever imagined. There is something about sexual sin which somehow 'feels dirtier' than other sin, I guess because people are involved directly. But God is sooooooo gracious and sooooooo loving, there is nothing he doesn't know and he is eager to accept us back! No matter what our minds will tell us, no matter what our friends will say, or what the devil will whisper to us, God is very happy and very willing to take us back no matter how dirty and full of crap we feel!

3. Make some sensible choices. Don't just read this next bit quickly but spend some time looking at it in detail. Think, pray, talk about it in a group of men or with someone you're accountable to. Advice like this can change your life.

Ten tips for maintaining sexual integrity

Tip 1: Get real

Recognise that sexual temptation is unavoidable in our sex-obsessed culture. Erotic images on billboards, films, television and a thousand other stimulants are bombarding you daily. Being a Christian doesn't exempt you from temptation – the godliest of men can fall prey to it. So the first step towards maintaining sexual integrity is to get real. Admit to yourself that sexual temptation is a problem that you have to reckon with. Remember John's warning: 'If we say that we have no sin, we deceive ourselves' (1 Jn. 1:8, NKJV).

Tip 2: Get serious

You should know by now that sexual sin ravages everyone connected with it. What you may not know is that every sexual fantasy you entertain, every flirtatious conversation you keep up, or every 'second look' you indulge in is the seed for AIDS, adultery, a broken heart, a shattered life. Get serious – if you're entertaining lust, you're dancing on a cliff. Take concrete action now while you can. 'Then, when desire has conceived, it gives birth to sin; and sin, when it is full-grown, brings forth death' (Jas. 1:15, NKJV).

Tip 3: Get ready

If you really believe an earthquake is coming some day, you prepare for it by developing an emergency plan. If you really believe sexual temptation is both common and can become lethal, you'll make an 'emergency plan' for it, too. Decide in advance what to do when you're tempted: how to distract yourself, who to call, how to escape close calls. Even St Paul admitted: 'I'm staying alert and in top condition. I'm not going to get caught napping, telling everyone else all about it and then missing out myself' (1 Cor. 9:27, The Message). Can you really afford to do less?

Tip 4: Get connected

Sexual sin thrives in the dark. If you're caught up in any sexual vice, one thing is certain: the secrecy surrounding your behaviour is what strengthens its hold on you. However ashamed you may feel about admitting your problem to another person, the reality is this: you can't overcome it on your own. If you could, wouldn't you have done so by now? Take a hint from James: 'Make this your common practice: Confess your sins to each other and pray for each other so that you can live together whole and healed. The prayer of a person living right with God is something powerful to be reckoned with' (Jas. 5:16, The Message). Find a trusted, mature Christian friend to confide in. Make that friend a partner in your recovery, and *never* assume that you've reached a point where you no longer need to be accountable.

Tip 5: Get brutal

I believe there's an eleventh commandment somewhere that says: 'Thou shalt not kid thy self.' If you're serious about sexual integrity, you'll distance yourself not only from the particular sexual sin you're most prone to (fantasising, pornography, affairs, prostitution) but you'll *also* distance yourself from any person or thing that entices you towards that sin. Sometimes, even a legitimate activity (certain movies, music or clubs, for example) may be OK for other people to indulge in, but not for you. Get brutally honest about your lifestyle: anything in it that makes you prone to sexual sin has to go. '"Everything is permissible for me" – but not everything is beneficial. "Everything is permissible for me" – but I will not be mastered by anything' (1 Cor. 6:12, NIV).

Tip 6: Get help

Sexual sins are often symptomatic of deeper emotional needs that a man is trying to satisfy in all the wrong ways. Repenting of the sin itself is a necessary first step, but recognising the conflicts or needs that led you into that behaviour may be the next step, requiring some specialised care from a Christian professional. Don't hesitate to seek godly counsel if you're trapped in cycles of ongoing, out-of-control behaviour. The answer you need may be more than just 'pray and get over it!'. King David (who was no stranger to sexual sin, by the way) found refuge in Samuel's wise mentoring (see 1 Sam. 19:18). If you're willing to seek professional help for taxes, medical care or career counselling, surely you'll be willing to do the same to maintain your sexual integrity?

Tip 7: Get comfortable
The problem of sexual temptation isn't going anywhere. It's been with us since time immemorial, and no doubt it will plague us until Christ comes. So get comfortable with the idea that you'll need to manage your sexual desires throughout life, always remembering that your sexual integrity is but a part of the general life-long sanctification process all Christians go through. 'I'm not saying that I have this all together, that I have it made', Paul told the Philippians. 'But I am well on my way, reaching out for Christ, who has so wondrously reached out for me. Friends, don't get me wrong: By no means do I count myself an expert in all of this, but I've got my eye on the goal, where God is beckoning us onward – to Jesus' (Phil. 3:12,13, The Message). So learn to love the process of pressing on, not perfection.

Tip 8: Get love
'I've been looking for love in all the wrong places', an old song laments. The sexual sin you're drawn towards may indeed be a cheap (though intense) substitute for love. You can repent of the sin, but not of the need the sin represents. So get love in your life: friendships, family, spouse, fellow believers. A man who truly loves, and knows he's truly

loved, is far less likely to search for what he already has in places he'll never find it. 'Why waste your money on what really isn't food? Why work hard for something that doesn't satisfy? Listen carefully to me, and you will enjoy the very best foods' (Is. 55:2, CEV). Learn to be intimate and authentic. It's one of the best ways to protect your heart and your integrity.

Tip 9: Get grace

It isn't the sinless man who makes it to the end, rather, it's the man who's learned to pick himself up after he stumbles. If your struggle seems relentless, remember this: when you commit yourself to sexual integrity, you commit yourself to a direction, not to perfection. You may stumble along the way – that's no justification for sin, just a realistic view of life in this fallen world. What determines the success or failure of an imperfect man is his willingness to pick himself up, confess his fault, and continue in the direction he committed himself to. Remember Paul's approach: 'I press on toward the goal to win the [supreme and heavenly] prize to which God in Christ Jesus is calling us upward' (Phil. 3:14, Amplified Bible).

Tip 10: Get a life

What's your passion? What's your calling? How clear are your goals? And, by the way, do you have any fun? The man who doesn't have a life – a passion, a sense of meaning, an ability to play as hard as he works – is a man with an emptiness tailor-made for sexual sin. Life is about more than keeping yourself sexually pure, as important as purity is. It's about knowing who and why you are, where your priorities lie, and where you're headed. If you don't know that much about yourself, you have some serious thinking to do. Commit yourself to developing your life as a good steward of your gifts and opportunities, and make that the context in which you seek to maintain your sexual integrity. Sexual integrity for its own sake is a good thing; sexual integrity for the sake of a higher calling is better. So by all means turn from your sin, but as you do, turn towards a goal-oriented, passionate, meaningful life. That is repentance in its truest, finest sense.[9]

Again, remember, you are not alone. It is just that some men haven't got the bottle to admit their failings in this way. I spoke to a man recently at a talk I did and he shared his experiences of addiction to Internet porn. He explained to the group that he is still tempted by it, but he is *very* accountable to someone now and he has come a long way. But he said that still 'it's a daily struggle' and perhaps that struggle wouldn't ever go away. The problem was so serious that he decided he didn't want a computer in his house, and he decided to remove that temptation completely. So if you have a serious addiction, radical steps may be needed; for many people there are ways of dealing with it through online accountability software and filtered ISPs, etc.[10]

And now the 'M' word!

Someone once said to me, 'Lee, most Christian leaders hope you won't ask the two questions: 1) How's your prayer life? and 2) Do you masturbate?' You won't hear that in an elders meeting very often!

So, the 'M' word, no it's not marriage or menstruation … we are talking about masturbation! Let's be clear, the Bible doesn't mention masturbation specifically. There is no proof text that I can quote to prove once and for all whether it's right or wrong. It is a personal doctrine issue, in other words you make a decision on it by taking into consideration the overview of the Bible and your relationship with God. That means it isn't a cut and dried answer that everyone would like. To make a straight 'it is wrong' decision, you would have to move firmly in legalism as there is no evidence for it in Scripture. We need to investigate it further.

A friend of mine once estimated how many times he had masturbated – and this had been a serious habit for him. The number was around 150,000 – no, it was, really! If the Victorians were right about their theories of the medical effects of masturbation, he must have contracted every disease known to mankind. He hasn't and they were wrong. It's embarrassing talking about it but 96 per cent of men have done it, and the other 4 per cent are probably lying. If we pretend it doesn't happen then we risk it becoming an unmentionable subject. But as me and Baz have started speaking at men's events, it is often the only issue that people want us to talk about! And it is the issue that they are expecting us to talk about, almost as if this is the only problem for men.

> I am fed up with books which just go on and on about masturbation. I wonder if, for some, reading books and hearing talks on masturbation is also an addiction.
>
> (A quote from an email I received from a UK church leader)

Focus

Masturbation and lust is a problem for many men but there are also other issues which are just swept under the carpet – money, abuse of power, control issues, pride and attitudes towards women are probably just as destructive for men as issues of lust. It is important that we don't focus all our teaching and indeed youth work on sex, lust and masturbation. There are many other issues that we can sharpen up on. It is very important that we don't get this one issue completely out of focus making it far more important than anything else in our lives – that's how guilt and hidden sin takes a hold. We need some balance.

> Don't knock masturbation – it's sex with someone
> I love.
>> (Woody Allen's character 'Alvy Singer'
>> from the film *Annie Hall*, United Artists, 1977)

Dr Steve Gerali has written a book called *The Struggle*.[11] It is a very honest and truthful account about his 25 years of experience in youth ministry. He deals with this issue in an honest and in-depth way and I would recommend you read it. In it he writes:

> ... to masturbate or not to masturbate that is the question and a good question. Each of us must formulate a personal view informed by factual evidence about sexuality and Scripture. Regardless of your viewpoint, there is freedom: freedom from guilt and shame, freedom to choose to engage or not and freedom from condemnation. Masturbation like all other wisdom issues, will provide one of three options for you:
> 1. You might call it sinful, in all cases
> 2. You might decide that it is an issue of personal liberty, within certain boundaries
> 3. You might see it as requiring continual discernment – because at times it may be right and at times it may be wrong.[12]

There is no doubt that the subject of masturbation is a grey issue and it does need discernment, discussion and honest accountability at times. Getting away from a Victorian view that masturbation was the cause of most modern illnesses is helpful, as is thinking about it in a more detached way with a biblical framework.

> I know nothing about sex because I was always married.
>
> (Zsa Zsa Gabor, US (Hungarian-born) actress)

Marriage isn't the answer!

I have spoken to many teenage lads over the years and whether it is pornography or masturbation, marriage is not the answer to their problems! It may even magnify an issue like masturbation, not solve it. It is important that you try and deal with it honestly and with wise people rather than blindly hoping that the desires will go away once you find a wife. This is also true for many other issues – marriage is great, but it is not a cure-all!

> The issue of masturbation cannot be regulated either by licence (anything goes) or by legalism (nothing allowed). No so-called proof text in the Bible indicates that masturbation is wrong, no proof text applies universal freedom to the issue either so this would indicate that masturbation is going to be a matter of personal conviction. For some it would be sin, for others it won't. Some of the key texts here for you to investigate further are ... Lev. 15:16–18, Rom. 1:24–27, 1 Cor. 7:9, Mt. 5:27,28, 1 Cor. 10:23.[13]

For groups and further study ...

Why not investigate this further and have a discussion with a couple of guys that you can be honest with?

There are loads of facts, figures, Bible verses and quotes to talk about in this chapter – revisit them honestly together. Openness breeds openness, someone has to bite the bullet and talk about it at some point – let it be you!

Your starters for ten ...

- You may not struggle with hardcore porn but what about late night TV?
- Is masturbation or fantasy the bigger issue? Discuss.

If you have been challenged by this chapter you are not alone. It is important that you talk to someone soon and admit that you do have a problem. Don't put it off.

There are further links and ways to find help on our website www.leeandbaz.com.

Notes

[1] Source: UK News, The *Telegraph*, NOP research group 1 July 2002.

[2] Choose your mail study October 1999.

[3] Source: MSNBC/Standford/Duquesne study 26 January 2000.

[4] *Christianity Today*, December 2002.

[5] *Christianity Today*, December 2001.

[6] Source: Cnet.com 28 April 1999.

[7] Source: AAP statement January 2001.

[8] From www.xxxchurch.com.

[9] Joe Dallas, Copyright 1999, used with kind permission. See www.pureonline.com and www.genesiscounseling.org

[10] See www.leeandbaz.com for more info on help that's available.

[11] Steve Gerali, *The Struggle*, Th1nk Books, NavPress Publishing Group, 2003. Used with kind permission.

[12] Steve Gerali, *The Struggle*, Th1nk Books, NavPress Publishing Group, 2003, page 162. Used with kind permission.

[13] Steve Gerali, *The Struggle*, Th1nk Books, Navpress Publishing Group, 2003, page 104. Used with kind permisssion.

'Everything is permissible for me' – but not everything is beneficial. 'Everything is permissible for me' – but I will not be mastered by anything.

(1 Cor. 6:12, NIV)

12

Get a Handle on It – Any Handle!

GAZ KISHERE

For the second time this week, I have had a 'bleeding hearts' session with one of my Christian friends who has, for want of a better phrase, 'shagged someone', although it was a surprise to find out this week that in some people's minds this is not necessarily seen as a shared role. Instead, such definitions as 'she shagged me' or 'I shagged him' made you somehow more or less involved. Sexually transmitted diseases are on the increase, is this why?

'I'm just hot blooded' may be true, but is no longer an acceptable covering statement for why we as men have such difficulties keeping the old fella locked in our underpants.

Yesterday, I had one of those email circulars about 'why women are better than men'. You know the kind of thing. This one was from a Christian lady and, sadly, it was like looking in a mirror (which I think was the idea). I liked this one best: 'A woman can manage to look at the opposite sex without imagining him naked.' How do they know this stuff? (Who let the cat out of the bag, that's what I'd like to know?)

Men *do* think about sex, perhaps not all of the time, but heck, a lot of it. All kinds of sex – some very down to earth, some way off the meter. We think about it, but as Christian men, rarely talk about it, and we should, because statistically we have as many issues with porn and immorality leading to broken relationships as any other men.

Where was I? Oh yes, getting a handle on it. The first time I said that to someone it was because he had gone to the dark side with a growing addiction to masturbation. I made the mistake of clenching my hand and shaking it at him, saying, 'You need to get a handle on it', after which we both wet ourselves laughing – but I think the imagery will have remained with him still to this day.

What was it that I didn't have a handle on, that allowed me to have sex with many girls I had worked with in my late teens and early twenties, that allowed me to have sex with someone else after I had begun to go out with my wife-to-be? What handles have I managed to get on the issue that have allowed me to stay 'shagging-others-free' since I have been married (18 years now)? I would like to say it was my wonderful wife, I should be saying it was my wonderful wife, but seven years into taking control of this area of my thinking as a married man, I had found several 'handles' to stop me crossing any lines – but still it wasn't this.

So, back to the guy I'd been speaking to today, my second 'I shagged so-and-so' or 'they shagged me' reference point of the week.

I asked him, 'What are you feeling?'

To which he replied, 'Remorse.'

To which I replied, 'Do you mean remorse, or do you mean self-pity because there is a difference, you see? Remorse means you are experiencing an internal conviction that something wrong has taken place, that you are beginning to take responsibility for it and that you are likely to find a "handle" which will help you not do it again. Pity, on the other hand, is not the same thing. Pity is you feeling bad for yourself, for the consequences of your action, for what the action has lost you – a partner maybe – or gained you – an infection or just an even more confused identity.'

Actually, it was a bit of both. I asked him what handle he could identify that would stop him crossing the line again.

He said, 'To be honest, I just feel I have given something of myself away, and that I am carrying something of her with me. I feel like we made a spiritual and emotional connection that wasn't right, that wasn't in the right place, the place of marriage where that kind of connecting has a safe place to be outworked – heck, I only met her last night.'

So, I just prayed for the guy, that God would gather him back to himself, that any unhealthy connection would be cut. He was after all genuinely sorry, for himself and for his friendship with God, as confused as his feelings and motives were.

It reminded me of myself and the timeline and processes I have had to deal with. For the first few years of my marriage, it wasn't my not wanting to get emotionally or spiritually connected to someone other than my wife that kept me on track. Another few years on, I grabbed a second handle, and this was a stronger one. I am a selfish person who had been thinking about the consequences of shagging around for myself, and suddenly I was thinking about what it meant for the other person, how it held them in their dysfunction, how it reinforced them getting their love deficits met in ways that could not satisfy or heal the gaps and wounds. Suddenly, I had woken up to compassion – the awareness of another. Suddenly, I woke up to what I had been doing to others. This was not loving others, this was not looking for the best in them, it was me taking what I wanted, regardless of them giving it freely – that is no justification at all. I think there is wisdom in a statement from the film *Vanilla Sky*[1] where a distraught and betrayed Julie (Cameron Diaz) turns to David (Tom Cruise) and says, 'When you sleep with someone, your body makes a promise – whether you do or not!' The issues of sex and the issues of our human and spiritual condition are deeper than we know.

That second handle saw me through a few more years. Man, we are such complex creatures it's no wonder we have no idea how to get things in the right order. I think God knows the complexity of our sexuality, and the complexity of our recovery into greater wholeness and fullness in him. Next? I have been a Christian since I was 18, and there, aged 30, I suddenly became sensitised to the fact that to walk down the 'pants down' road also affects my friendship with Jesus, who wants the best for me and has to endure watching on the sidelines where I've thrown him (or out of mind/out of sight), putting yet more stuff that blocks my intimacy with him. Yes, and eventually, in the mess of the process and my own recovery of self through God's healing, my beautiful wife comes into view – how could I ever do anything like that to her? I had focused in on sex and the act of intercourse, but we give ourselves away in a great many other ways to people, ways that keep us and others broken and stuck in self-depreciating cycles – sex is just one of the things we need to get a handle on.

I've now kept my tail between my legs for 18 years of marriage. Did I have my order right? Probably not. Did I have my priorities right? *Yes* – 'Don't do it, Gaz; get a handle on it – any handle – just find one!' God knows the intentions of our hearts. Even if we still have things to wrestle with, he will wrestle with us till we break through, until we get a handle, heck, get a few, but start somewhere.

- What relationships are most likely to be affected by giving into sexual brokenness?
- What issues of worth and identity are likely to be negatively reinforced for you and for the other person involved?
- People tend to sexualise their unmet love needs, love and affirmation deficits from childhood, attempting to find an instant fix through sexual encounters. Has it worked? Is it likely to ever really work?
- What's really going to meet those love needs? Love? Is pursuit of sex outside of the safe setting of marriage likely to change issues of brokenness, or hold you in them?
- What's your 'handle'?
- Have you given yourself away to others? Do you carry others with you to this day? Do you need to ask God to 'gather' you back to yourself emotionally and spiritually?

http://emergensee.blogspot.com

Note

[1] *Vanilla Sky*, Paramount Pictures, 2001.

I saw that show '50 things to do before you die'
– I would have thought the obvious one was
'Shout for help'.

(Mark Watson)

13

Missionary? ... Me?

IAN WILSON[1]

Ian was one of the men that inspired us to write *Dead Men Walking* and start this mad journey into the world of honest manhood! He is a normal bloke who is a constant inspiration to me and Baz so we asked him to write a bit for you lot and he emailed it from Africa – when the electricity was on! (Lee and Baz)

Shocker

After three and a half hours in a truck that had never possessed a shock absorber in its life, driving through a Tanzanian pothole, loosely termed a road, we arrived at the orphanage to meet the 'missionary sisters'. During our journey, my missionary 'sister' stereotype had gone into overdrive: 350 years old, hair in a bun, jam-jar glasses, front teeth that walked in front of you, sandals with white ankle socks (that went nowhere near the ankle) and whispering the name of Jesus 'lest we offendeth'! Thankfully, the sisters were anything but my appalling stereotype and even more thankfully I married one of them – Andie (Andrea ... she's a girl by the way!) – 18 months later.

As I write, I now live in Tanzania, in a place called Mwanza. Mwanza is a city sitting on the edge of Lake Victoria and consists of some 700,000 people, but a regional population of approximately 13 million across eleven districts. To some, I am 'the missionary' but for me I am simply a bloke who loves Jesus and wants to take steps of faith and risk to follow him. My mate, J. John, says this, 'A missionary is not someone who crosses the sea but is someone who has seen the cross!' Seeing the cross for us as a family has brought us to Tanzania but we are still ordinary people allowing our extraordinary God to use us to make a difference in the lives we touch daily here. For you it may involve your neighbour, your town, your city. Where you are now.

I am a dentist and an evangelist ... a unique combination if ever there was one – 'This won't hurt a bit, sir! Especially if you give your life to Jesus ... NOW!' Andie and I lead an NGO (non-governmental organisation) called Bridge2aid, where the dental centre we have opened generates the income we use to plough back into the training of Tanzanian primary healthcare workers to take out teeth safely in remote areas of the country. We also fund the provision of food, medical care and clothing to the poor and homeless communities or 'Maskini' of the city. These are the untouchables of society here, those who with HIV/leprosy/disabilities have had their dignity, self-worth, creativity and friendship stripped from them. People should never have to live this way and it makes us angry that they have to, often through no fault of their own. My family and I are ordinary people who are here because we have seen the cross and the difference that an extraordinary God can make with us and through us for the benefit of others.

People have said to us, 'Oh you are so brave to do what you do!' You cannot imagine how scared I was as we got ready to come here and then as we settled here. I have to say that Andie was much more together and 'cool' about the whole process. There were times when what we were doing seemed crazy, mad and irresponsible but God had called us and we had no choice but to discover what his call meant for us and to go. How long will we be here? I have no idea but I don't want to move on to the next stage of our adventure with Jesus until he clearly says so.

As you read this I want to encourage you that God has an amazing destiny over your life. It is unique to you and you alone. It will not be easy and there will be the highs and the lows but it is part of your identity and make up and should you avoid it, pass it up or ignore it, I believe that you will always feel that there is something missing.

For all of us men with our hopes, dreams, fears, joys and failures, let's not shrink from our destiny or the call to be men of faith, risk and dare ... even if we don't feel like being one!

Questions

- What can you do?
- And what can you do now?!
- What are you good at?
- What do you enjoy?
- Who do you know?

Ordinary questions, yes! But the lives of the many people around you depend on you giving your ordinary answers into the hands of an extraordinary God.

Missionary? Cross the sea to serve God? Maybe one day, until then make sure you see the cross where you are now.

Dad

Six weeks ago I travelled to the UK to be with Andie and the kids as our third child was due to be born. The skies above Heathrow welcomed me on that 11 June with a beautiful sunny morning, and even the British Airways ground staff seemed to have collectively swallowed 'happy to help' pills that day.

I was to fly straight up to Newcastle and then go to see Dad who had been in several nursing homes since his stroke in 2003 and Mum's death in November 2004. Basil Charles Wilson just 'wanted to go home to be with Jesus and be at peace' and every time I had seen him he had asked, 'Can you put a good word in, son, with Jesus, to get my room in the mansion ready?' A man of quiet, personal faith he was my hero, pouring himself out sacrificially for the life of his only often unappreciative son (that's me by the way!). I am the only child for Mum and Dad as the tragedy of miscarriage had robbed them of the children they craved on several occasions.

Once I had arrived at the nursing home, the Wilson family and friends sat around him and went into action! Laughing, cracking jokes with him and holding his hand. His physical limitations were evident but the life and character still shone through.

Later, as we left after having had several fun-filled hours together, I hugged him close saying, 'Love you Dad.' 'Love you, too,' came his reply. I kissed him on the cheek goodbye ... it was to be the last time we would do this. The next morning, 'his room must have been ready' and Jesus took him home.

Nursing staff later told me that Dad had been saying, 'I'll wait to see Ian and then I will go.' The fact that God allowed us to have those few hours together having 'fallen off' a ten-hour flight was a grace moment for me. On 12

June 2005 Dad went 'home'; 15 July 2005 our third child Neema Grace Wilson was born.

Life! Problem-free please with a guarantee of no pain or suffering! I would like the ecstasy of celebrating the birth of Jake, Imani and Neema every day please!

We all know that life is not like that, celebration and pain in various measures is the cocktail of day-to-day living and Jesus never promised us the pain-free variety but he did reassure us that he knew what we were going through and he promised he would never leave us to go through it alone.

My experience is that the peace and the grace of the Lord really doesn't hit home until I am in the circumstances when I really need his peace and grace in my life.

My birth certificate tells me I am a son by natural birth. My Bible tells me I am a son by spiritual birth (Rom. 8:15). I still have a dad ... I am not an orphan. As a son of God the Father, I want to celebrate the life he graciously gives me and, when the pain and suffering comes, to understand and continue to live in the knowledge that Jesus, God's kid, 'familiar with suffering', has been there, literally to hell and back, for me!

Questions

- When did you last honour your dad and mum, or simply tell them that you love and appreciate them?
- Have you come to know the reality of God being your dad no matter how good or bad your earthly dad was/is?
- What pain or suffering are you going through right now? Have you been able to talk it through with close friends? I encourage you to do so. Tell them honestly how you feel.

- Are you angry or confused as to where God was in your pain? Please forgive the cliché but He *does* understand and he *has* been there before you and though you may not realise it now he *still* stands there with you. I hope that in time you can allow him to bring healing and understanding to your pain.

www.bridge2aid.org

Note

[1] Or 'Jocky' as we know him!

Shall I abandon, O King of mysteries, the soft
  comforts of home?
Shall I turn my back on my native land, and turn
  my face towards the sea?
Shall I put myself wholly at your mercy,
without silver, without a horse,
without fame, without honour?
Shall I throw myself wholly upon you,
without sword and shield, without food and
  drink,
without a bed to lie on?
Shall I say farewell to my beautiful land, placing
  myself under your yoke?
Shall I pour out my heart to you, confessing my
  manifold sins and begging forgiveness,
tears streaming down my cheeks?
Shall I leave the prints of my knees on the sandy
  beach,
a record of my final prayer in my native land?
Shall I then suffer every kind of wound that the
  sea can inflict?
Shall I take my tiny boat across the wide
  sparkling ocean?
O King of the Glorious Heaven, shall I go of my
  own choice upon the sea?
O Christ, will you help me on the wild waves?

(Ascribed to Saint Brendan the Navigator
  before sailing across the Atlantic)

14

Really Small Jesus

ANDY FLANNAGAN

As a man, I often struggle from being too flippin' good at being efficient. It makes me feel good, but it is often eternally worthless. Unfortunately, the Jesus I know is still smaller than the Jesus I don't yet know.

Recently, I was on holiday on the north coast of Northern Ireland. It is probably one of my favourite parts of the whole world, but my ability to fully appreciate its crashing waves and jutting headlands was seriously diminished by the fact that on the day before arriving, about £500 had been stolen from my CD stall at a concert. On the day afterwards, I don't think it would have made much difference to me whether I was in the slums of Bangladesh or the Hanging Gardens of Babylon, as the greens were greyed, the sounds were muted and the clouds were darkened. Nothing about my state of mind changed the reality of what lay before me. The beaches had not shortened, the cliffs had not shrunk, and the sea had not become suddenly polluted. What had changed was my ability to appreciate the reality before me without prejudice. The same applies to our ability to come before the reality of who Jesus is. Yes, we must bring all our frustrations and dilemmas to him, but if we are always preoccupied, as we tend to be, are we truly experiencing him as he really is, or a version tainted by our current foibles and mindset? We may miss something of his beauty that is there to be seen. With our current agenda firmly in the forefront of our minds it is very easy for self-interest to manipulate our image of his character onto the true picture of God.

This is how I know that there is still so much more to know of this Jesus. My preoccupation with my agenda leaves just enough space to remember 'What Would Jesus Do?' in any given situation, but leaves absolutely no room to see or to ask the more important question – 'What is Jesus doing?' When I speak to my peers, I realise that this is not just a problem for me. We think 'Jesus thoughts' when we pray about the future and when we say thanks for the past, but we have practically no awareness of Jesus in the 'now'. How can we truly be his co-workers, when we only spot what he has been up to a day or so later, after the dust settles? Right now, ask yourself the question – what is Jesus doing in my life, in this situation, in this town, or in this family right *now*? Because I can assure you of one thing, he is always doing something. The question is whether or not our preoccupied minds leave us the space to see it.

When I wake up, I am already thinking through my 'to-do list' for the day. That is reality. That is 'sorting things' and calling people, and having meetings. The problem is that often this is my only reality. The great French philosopher Descartes said, 'I think, therefore I am.' In other words, we know that we are real because we can feel ourselves thinking. I am sure that one of the main reasons that as a society we seem to care little for anyone other than ourselves is that to us, everyone else is genuinely less real, as we simply cannot 'hear' their thinking. Can you hear Jesus 'thinking'? Is there space in your head to be filled with thoughts other than your own? 'Is he slightly less real than reality?'

My closest friends are those with whom I don't have to organise an 'event' to have a good time. No excuse is required to be in their company. I can be with them and just 'be'. In these times, I truly begin to *know* them, as I am investing my brain not in a flurry of activity, but in looking and listening. With these folks, I begin to be able to anticipate their bodily reaction to a surprise, the tone their voice will take in response to provocation, or what will make them laugh. My desire is that I will begin to know my Jesus in the same way. That as with the prophets, I will not only know of his actions and reactions in history, but how he is thinking, acting and reacting right now.

I think Jesus wants to speak into more situations in our world than we suspect. I think he has a view on everything that we get involved in.

A good example of our tunnel vision is in the area of politics. I recently received an email from a friend in the USA. It said a very interesting thing: 'Yes, I agree that Bush's foreign policy is questionable, but I still prefer him to Kerry on moral issues.' When did Jesus and morality become separate from foreign policy? This dichotomy is also rampant in the business sector. What would Jesus have to say about that accounting practice, or that marketing strategy? Or do we only let Jesus have his say on our personal 'spiritual lives'.

The Jesus I know caused trouble, and to be honest we in the West seem to have designed our lives to avoid it at all costs. Jesus spoke directly to people, but in pleasant Christian circles, we'd rather talk to 'Tom, Dick and Harry' about an offence, and the person with whom we have a grievance is often the last to hear about it. As the proverb says, 'As iron sharpens iron, so one man sharpens another' (Prov. 27:17, NIV).

Here are some more things about the Jesus I know. But remember, like you, I haven't seen all of him yet, and that's my fault not his, so any falsehood here is mine. I'd know he'd want me to be provocative, even if I didn't get everything right ...

> The Jesus I know would condemn abortion, but comfort those who have gone through it.

> The Jesus I know would never put a nation's interests above the interests of the kingdom.

> The Jesus I know would scream at a world economic system that rapes the developing world.

> The Jesus I know would support Liverpool FC. Oops, I think I just made my point.

> This is the Jesus I am still getting to know.

www.andyflan.com

When I look at the blood all I see is love, love,
   love.
When I stop at the cross I can see the love of
   God

But I can't see competition
I can't see hierarchy
I can't see pride or prejudice or the abuse of
   authority
I can't see lust for power
I can't see manipulation
I can't see rage or anger or selfish ambition.

But I can't see unforgiveness
I can't see hate or envy
I can't see stupid fighting or bitterness, or
   jealousy.
I can't see empire building
I can't see self importance
I can't see back stabbing or vanity or arrogance.

I see surrender, sacrifice, salvation,
Humility, righteousness, faithfulness, grace,
   forgiveness.
Love, Love, Love ... Love, Love, Love.
When I Stop! ... at the cross
I can see the love of God.

15

Life or Death?

BAZ GASCOYNE

I'm always amazed how calm people seem when they are retelling their near-death experiences. Whether they have been struck by lightning whilst playing golf, attacked by a killer shark or crocodile, or survived an aeroplane crash, they tell the news reporter as if it was just like going to buy a loaf of bread from the local shop!

A few years ago, whilst on holiday in Florida, I was doing the man thing – I was in charge of the TV remote control and was surfing the six billion channels that they have over in the States rather than the five we have at home.

I came across the Ricki Lake show and was amazed at what was beginning to unfold on the screen. The theme of the show was something like 'reunited' but was strange as it was not with old school or college loves but with people who had been bullied by the guests on the show. So, try to imagine the scenario. Ricki introduced the first guest who walked on to huge raptures of cheers, whistles and applause. He waved to the audience and sat down. Ricki and the guest exchanged polite pleasantries. Remember, he had no idea why he was on the show apart from knowing someone from school wanted to meet up again after all these years. 'Dwain' (not his real name), about 29 years old, sat looking cool in his denims and tight-fitting T-shirt, dark hair and Colgate smile.

'So, Dwain, have you any idea who from high school might want to meet up with you after all these years?'

'Not at all,' he replied with a smile and a glint in his eyes. Ricki and he talked about past girlfriends, life at school and whether there was any bullying, and still Dwain had no idea who wanted to meet him. Eventually, Ricki asked for a huge photo of the mystery guest to be lowered from the studio ceiling. The crowd began to whistle and cheer as the photo of a beautiful young lady in her late twenties was lowered. She looked to be about 6 feet tall, elegant in a stunning red dress showing off her figure, beautiful blue eyes, a stunning smile and thick wavy blonde shoulder-length hair.

Eventually, Ricki got the audience to quieten down and Dwain said he had no idea who she was, but would like to meet her.

Ricki then asked for a photo of the mystery lady as she looked at school to be lowered. Dwain, the audience and I were on the edge of our seats as the photo was lowered of a girl aged about 14. She was tall, quite plump, with tight curly blond hair, two large front teeth and large glasses.

The crowd gasped, I shouted 'No way!' and Dwain looked pale. It was obvious he remembered her. When asked, he gave her name but said he hadn't had anything to do with her. 'Wow that's strange considering you remembered her name.' Ricki had just served an ace. I was feeling uncomfortable sat in my friend's lounge thanking God it was not me having to go through this ordeal. Imagine if we had to go through this with all the people we had ever bullied or gossiped about? Now he is looking like someone has poured itching powder down the back of his shirt and inside his Calvin Klein boxer shorts. 'Is there anything you want to say, Dwain?' After what seemed ages, probably only 30 seconds, he nervously and quietly admitted it was the girl he used to bully. The crowd jeered in a holier-than-thou kind of way and they rose to their feet pointing fingers and fists in his direction.

Once again Ricki had to do her headmistress imperson-ation and tell the badly behaved class to quieten it. She then turned to Dwain who now looked more like a nervous schoolboy sitting outside the head teacher's office than a cool 29-year-old, and the conversation went something like this: 'Why did you bully her?'

'For a bit of a laugh to look good in front of my mates.'

'So what did you do?'

'You know, call her names.'

'Like what?'

'Goofy, Bugs Bunny, Mop head, Jam jars, shitty.'

The audience were back on their feet baying for blood. Ricki asked how his victim responded to his verbal attacks.

'She used to look upset at times but it was only a bit of fun.'

'Did you ever stop to think what damage it might have caused her whilst this was going on?'

'Nah, we didn't mean anything by it.'

The crowd began to get hysterical as Ricki got ready to introduce the girl in the photos. There was music and flashing lights as the stunning lady in the red dress bursts through the photo and confidently walked on stage. As the studio audience quietened down, and she sat in the chair next to Dwain, the only thing I could hear was my heart pounding with the tension. And 'Charmaine' as we will call her (not her real name) began to tell Dwain of the devastating effect his verbal bullying had had on her life, and the two years of counselling she had needed to work through the pain and cancel out the destructive words that had been spoken to her. And then, an electrifying moment as Dwain, looking shamefaced and misty eyed, apologised and asked for forgiveness, and Charmaine said she already had but thanked him for his apology. There was not a dry eye in the studio, or on the settee as I sat, a blubbering wreck, in my friend's lounge in Florida.

Charmaine then explained that she was working as a youth counsellor, visiting high schools to expose the dangers of bullying. A commercial break was announced and I decided I couldn't take anymore and turned the TV off, silently considering the dangers of what comes out of my mouth.

There is an old proverb that says: 'The tongue has power to give life or destroy it.' How true that is.

I thought back to my last year at junior school when our teacher announced the joyous activity of writing about what we had done over the summer holiday. Its purpose? To help the school assess which form we would be in when we left and went to the 'big' school. The school I went to was wonderful. I thoroughly enjoyed being there. However, the political-correctness crew would have a field day at how they used to have the classroom set out. The tables were set in such a way that whoever walked in could immediately assess a pupil's 'status' by which table they were sat on. So the first table was for the wazzerks, then the blebs, then the semi-blebs, below average, average, above average, swots, mega swots, creeps, and then the 'don't talk to them' table. Well, I was proudly sat on the first table with my mates – we were the people the school didn't expect to achieve anything. When you have a system in place like this, automatically you take on the persona that is expected of you. So whenever another teacher or pupil entered the classroom you knew they were scanning the room from left to right to see where everyone was sat. Lovely!

Anyway, back to the story. We were given our exercise books and told to get on with our work. I can't remember what I wrote but it didn't seem long before we were handing our books in and going out for break to play football. After lunch, back in the classroom, our teacher informed us he had had a chance to look at the work. There had been some excellent work looking to the 'don't talk to them' table; some very good work (creeps and mega swots table); some good work (swots and above average table); and some OK work (average and below average table). It seemed that his tone of voice slowly changed to a more deliberate and slow sound as he expressed his disapproval of the standard of work. Once he was looking towards the last three tables you could see the frustration in his eyes and voice. 'There has been some poor work' (semi-blebs and blebs table) and then 'there has been some abysmal work' (wazzerks with yours truly). He then went on to draw everyone's attention to a piece of work he had written out on the board, as an example of how not to write a story. I don't remember his exact words but something along the lines of the spelling being atrocious, punctuation poor and the whole thing being useless. All along I knew that he was making fun of my work, but when others laughed at the mistakes so did I as I did not want people to know that it was mine. But it wasn't long before the class had to stop trying to guess whose work it was as our teacher decided to help them.

He asked for the person whose work this was to stand up. So, as everyone was looking around, I stood, and as others smiled I began to smile to try and hide the hurt I was feeling inside. My memory of what followed had an effect on my life for over 30 years. 'Son, I don't know why you are smiling. This work is pathetic. Why do you bother to come to school? You are as thick as two short planks and will never achieve anything in your life.' The class was laughing and I began to laugh and sway like a weeble, but inside I was feeling angry and wishing I could punch or head-butt him in the nuts. But I was only 10 or 11 years old. I do need to say that he was a good teacher. I enjoyed being in his class most of the year and had liked him until this point. I still have many good memories of him and the class. I'm not sure if he's just had a bad day or week, or maybe his wife was not allowing him to have sex, but whatever it was I got the brunt of it that day.

So as the old proverb says, 'The tongue has power to give life or destroy it.'

I have told that story in many schools over the years as well as in men's meetings or church meetings. No matter where I tell it I always have people coming up to me telling me a similar thing happened to them. Teachers who went in to teaching to nurture the young and end up doing the opposite; grown men crying as they retell what their fathers said to them. Many people have been hurt by the spoken word, so as I retell this story, I also tell of the things I have been able to achieve in the last few years as I have allowed God to touch that area of my life with his love, heal the negative words and remove the curse spoken over my life.

I know in the past I have caused hurt to other people through things I have said to them. Hurt people hurt people. The more you and I allow God to heal our hurts the less we will hurt others.

My desire is to bring words of life, hope and healing; words that build up and encourage. I know I don't always succeed but I know it's far better than the alternative of death.

This August we read in most of the national papers that the Revised Oxford Dictionary has 350 words to hurt and just 40 expressions to praise and encourage. 'Human nature being what it is, perhaps it's not surprising there are more words to convey negative feelings than positive ones,' said one expert at publisher Oxford University Press.

It's easy to be negative – let's be people who speak words of life to people not death, and begin to change society.

To ponder on

- Careless words stab like a sword but wise words bring healing.
- As a tree gives fruit, healing words give life but dishonest words crush the spirit.
- Pleasant words are like honeycomb, making people happy and healthy.
- What you say can mean life or death.

All these proverbs are taken from the Bible. Just maybe God knows what he is talking about.

Questions

- Do your words bring life or death to those around you? What about those who are closest to you?
- Are any incidents of death-giving words from your past still with you that you need to allow God to heal and redeem?

Complete the following sentence: 'Church notice boards are ...'

16

Surely Not?

BILLY PRINCE

It's not very often you hear the audible voice of God, but when it happened to me, God spoke exactly like me dad would.

It was at the end of Art Attack[1] in 1994. This had been one of the most difficult and challenging four or five days of my life. I'd learned a lot about how I felt about myself, how I saw myself and about how I wanted others to see me. On the final evening, Gerald Coates turned up to pray with us. I was delighted, expectant and very nervous when Gerald turned towards me and started to pray. He put his outstretched hand on my chest and I 'went doon like a sack of tatties' (which means I hit the ground very heavily as if someone had dropped a bag of potatoes). It was the first time that I'd really been 'slain in the Spirit'. I had lain down before after people had prayed with me, but this was the first time I'd actually been knocked off my feet.

And that's when it happened. God spoke in an audible voice. As I lay there, it was as if I was outside on a grassy hillside and covered in layers and layers of heavy blankets. God showed me that each blanket was a concern or worry that I was carrying. As I lay there, unable to move or hardly breathe, I felt God take a blanket, identify what it stood for and whisk it high into the sky, where it soared completely out of view. As he did this he said, 'Don't worry about that, son, that's not your concern, in fact, don't you give a bugger. Don't give a bugger about it.'

It was great for me to hear this. It completely cracked me up. I laughed so much that I wasn't just in tears I was in agony. I was laughing so hard I thought I was going to do some permanent damage. I was wishing, begging God to stop, but wanting the whole thing to continue, which it did. Each blanket, each concern off high, high into the clear sky and God's voice loud and clear, 'Don't give a bugger, son.'

Now I know that some of you at this point might want to put this down and not read any more. I mean, come on, God swearing? It can't be right! But before you do, let me explain.

I'm a Geordie, brought up in an un-churched family in the middle of industrial Tyneside. My dad (my earthly, very earthly dad) was a miner, a face worker in the local colliery and swearing was a natural part of my upbringing. Not heavy, sexual swearing, but I suppose what I would consider as normal everyday stuff. Bugger and bloody and stuff like that. In the back lane and at school, everybody swore at you, including some of the teachers.

So you see, when God spoke, and swore, to me, and I forgot to mention, in a Geordie accent (now that probably really is heresy), it showed to me in a very, very real way that he really was my dad. Not just in an airy-fairy, God is your father sort of way, but in a kind of 'Howay, son, let's sort this out for you' way, in a me and you, flesh to flesh, spirit to spirit way.

I don't think for a minute that God's a Geordie or that he has to swear to get close to us. But that's what he did for me, because he knew that was how he'd get through to me. Coming down to my level to bring me up to his and that's how special and great and glorious God is. That's how much he values a father/son, father/daughter relationship with all of us. For me, he reached down right to my level to raise me up to be nearer to him.

> Most English people's goal in life is to get to the grave without ever being embarrassed.
>
> (John Cleese)

Note

[1] A conference for artists and media people.

Ask people about God nowadays and they usually reply, 'I'm not religious, but deep down I'm a very spiritual person.' What this phrase really means is, 'I'm afraid of dying but I can't be arsed going to church.'

(Colin Ramone)

17

Michael Jordan's Light Bulb

LEE JACKSON

Thomas Edison: 'father of the modern world' (1847–1931). 'No one did more to share the physical character of our present day civilisation ... he was the most influential figure of the Millennium.'[1]

One of Thomas Edison's 1,093 inventions was the light bulb filament, but it took him over 3,000 attempts to invent it! That means 2,999 attempts at getting it to work, failed. He worked 18-hour days and only had five hours' sleep a night. He said to his friends, 'I don't even need exercise, I don't need to play golf because I have all the exercise I need going from one lab to another.'

In a similar vein, in my opinion Michael Jordan may be the greatest sports star of all time. He won six NBA world titles – the most valuable player in all of them. He won the NBA slamdunk contest twice, changing it for ever. He scored 32,292 points in his career. He was, unlike many players these days, 'the complete package': he had the greatest offence, stifling defence and he was a media phenomenon, doing feature films through to cereal adverts. Yet he said this: 'I have missed more than 9,000 shots in my career. I have lost almost 300 games. Twenty-six times I have been trusted to take the game-winning shot and have missed; I have failed over and over and over again in my life and that is why I succeed.'

Somehow, in this instant world of Pot Noodles, McDonald's and quick boiling kettles, where the National Lottery promises us the ultimate get rich quick scheme and we respond to spam emails believing that someone has left us £2 million if we could only send them £100 for an administration fee(!), the concept that failure strengthens us has been lost. Often, it is in failure that we learn to succeed.

Paul says, '... I don't understand why I act the way I do. I don't do what I know is right. I do the things I hate' (Rom. 7:15, CEV) but he also says, 'My friends, I don't feel that I have already arrived. But I forget what is behind, and I struggle for what is ahead. I run toward the goal, so that I can win the prize of being called to heaven. This is the prize that God offers because of what Christ Jesus has done ... But we must keep going in the direction that we are now headed' (Phil. 3:13,14,16, CEV).

Genius is 1 per cent inspiration and 99 per cent perspiration.

So next time you switch on a bulb in your house remember Thomas Edison and all his failures, the difficulties and the struggles that he had to overcome to become the man that he was to be. And next time you see a basketball, imagine Michael Jordan being gutted 26 times after missing his game-winning shot, when he was the best player in the world.

Remember that God didn't tell us that we would succeed easily and avoid suffering, he just said that he would be there with us. That makes *all* the difference.

Note

[1] *The Heroes of the Age – Electricity and Man.*

The best church noticeboard ever?

'God bless our troops overseas. Sign vandals are the scum of the earth.'

18

Understanding Integrity

LEE JACKSON

Men occasionally stumble over the truth, but most of them pick themselves up and hurry off as if nothing ever happened.

(Sir Winston Churchill, British politician)

An African minister came to the UK to do a series of Bible studies in a church. He brought some Powerpoint presentations to use with his talks but his technology wasn't up to date, so he brought them on an old style 5½" floppy disk. In Africa, they call those disks 'floppies' and they call the 3½" disks we use 'stiffies'. The church had an old computer and was able to copy these disks onto 3½" disks. He was very very grateful as his notes had been saved and his technology was ready! At the end of the week, he was giving his thank-yous for 'how kind' everyone had been during the week. He stood up to thank everyone and he mentioned Jean, the woman who had helped him with his computer problem. He stood at the front of the church and said, 'I would just like to thank Jean for the amount of stiffies that she has given me this week.' As you can imagine there were various reactions.

Some people were silently appalled and offended by the mere mentioning of such things and at the end the pastor was told to go and speak to him about this issue. The pastor said to this guy that he had said 'something offensive' but he was so embarrassed he couldn't come round to saying what it was that had offended everybody. Instead he just vaguely told him off and they went their separate ways.

It is amazing that the local pastor said that he had been offended and yet didn't specify why that was; and this other guy, in complete innocence and complete integrity, mentioning his stiffies. English lunacy and, if you'll pardon the pun, an example of our stiff upper lip!

Cultural differences make for some interesting moments! Yet this African pastor had complete integrity out of pure naïvety. Some would say that we cannot be naïve any more. I would have to agree. We have to decide that we cannot be naïve, or even worse, we cannot appear to be naïve. It is time that we really stepped up and tried to understand what genuine integrity is. In this chapter, I'm going to spell out a few things that I have noticed when doing men's work.

Life isn't very straight forward, and the last couple of years have certainly been quite difficult for me. Yet still in these times we have to try to maintain our integrity the best that we can – to be the people that we project. To be the people that we say we are. It's probably one of the most uncomfortable things a man can do.

Abuse

Unfortunately, the word 'integrity' has been thrown around in many Christian men's events and has become a slightly odd, patriarchal word which somehow has been made to mean control over your family, your friends and your workplace. That is not what it is meant to be. A great example of this is in Mt. 21 when Jesus enters the temple. He gets angry in the temple over the people selling stuff. He throws the tables over and shouts, really disrupting things, yet he does that with complete integrity, not only because he is the Son of God, but also because he was able to say to people 'look at my life' and 'look at what I am about'. In order for the passion and anger to rise up in him at that point, integrity was central to his power. He was who he said he was, plain and simple. In fact, just before that incident people shouted who he was as he entered Jerusalem on a donkey, and afterwards he healed people! And those who he healed were probably being kicked out of the temple by the priests anyway. His anger was not a call to 'look at me' but a prophetic statement to the religious leaders. There was true justice in this scene.

So how do we survive this crazy life?

One of the first things to remember is that our faith is a journey and it is not a set of principles that we live by. This whole sense of journeying with God has really been lost in modern Christianity. If you have ever seen the film *Saved*[1] featuring Mandy Moore you will understand. In it, a right wing Christian college have a hard set of rules which everyone has to follow. They have forgotten that instead they should be journeying with God, not be in love with the rules that they think he gives, or even worse add their own twist to them. At one point, one of the young people starts to question her faith so they try to kidnap her and exorcise her of her 'demons' – she was just questioning a few things, but that did not fit into their religious regime.

Dual

We are simply walking with God. Sometimes we walk closely with him, sometimes we have got our back turned to him (and that makes it really difficult to walk!). Sometimes he seems distant but we are still walking with him. I think the Celtic saints showed us how to journey and walk with God very clearly. As we journey, the key to survival is understanding that we are under attack: the world, the devil, people around us are out to attack us in various ways. Always looking for the lowest common denominator, looking for common ground. Telling us we should buy everything we want because we deserve it, telling us that we should see as much porn as we can because we deserve it. We are men and it doesn't affect our lives. We should spend our money how we want to, deal with our businesses in the way that we want to. All this stuff is thrown at us every day and we need to be ready for constant attack. The number one thing that is attacked is the 'real you' and one of the biggest problems that we have today is the survival mechanism of what I have called dualism. It certainly is a major problem for some people in their teens and twenties in particular. When I was growing up, if I had done something wrong, then I was enormously guilty about it. I would feel guilty and sorry, apologising to God a thousand times and eventually coming back to God, half letting it go and then trying to get on with my life. The following is a classic example.

I shot the sheriff but I didn't shoot the deputy!

When I was in my rap group, H.O.G. in the nineties with my great friends Justin, Matt and Nick, we were travelling to a gig in this van that someone from church had lent us. It was one of those vans that had been converted – there was storage space and big comfy bucket seats. It even had a mobile phone before many people had mobiles. It was very exciting! We went travelling in the van to somewhere in the south, enjoying every bump of the M1 that we got to know so well. I was driving at the time and everyone in the back of the van got really bored so they decided that it would be funny to start messing about with our water pistol props. Unfortunately, the water pistols were in the shape of .45 hand guns. It was around the time of the beginning of gangster rap and Nick thought it would be 'really funny' to fire water at oncoming vehicles as we drove. So we were going down a country road trying to find our gig. As cars came past us he leant out of the window with this replica hand gun and started squirting water at the oncoming traffic.

I had no idea this was happening but obviously it really freaked out the drivers of oncoming cars. We were driving along a bit further and I suddenly realised a police car had pulled in behind us. I thought he was just checking us out, whatever. So I just kept going, then a police car pulled in front of us so we were hemmed in between two top-of-the-range traffic cars. Suddenly, the one in front started to brake hard with his blue lights on. He forced us to pull in to a lay-by. I had to slam on the brakes and pull over. The van was an A-team style van with a side sliding door, so we opened the door and the police shouted in a megaphone style, 'COME OUT OF THE VAN WITH YOUR HANDS UP!', and 'STEP AWAY FROM THE VAN!' We all got out and they went inside the van and picked up, with a pencil, like only policemen could, the offending water pistol which looked like a real gun. The policeman held it up and asked, 'Whose is this?' Justin admitted it was his (but it was actually Nick that was doing the shooting!). I think the police probably thought it was quite funny. They gave the lads a stern telling off and put us back in the van and thankfully didn't arrest or shoot us.

Of course we were going to 'serve the Lord' at the time so we didn't mention this at the gig and we didn't mention it at church either. That is until Justin based his whole best man speech around it! People from church were supporting us financially, lending us this van, praying for us and then we nearly got arrested for carrying a firearm that we aimed at oncoming traffic! It was awful at the time and I wish we had admitted it quickly to everyone at church but I was scared of the kickback at the time and so I just felt guilty about it for ages! Trying to forget it ever happened – with Justin and Nick reminding me of it at every opportunity they could.

But now it seems that with teens and twenties dualism is a massive problem and feeling the kind of guilt that I just described is less and less common.

But what is it?

In order to survive this mad life, some people manage to 'put their lives in little boxes'. There is a box which has all their church stuff in it, there is a box for work and there is a box for money and finances. There is also a box that has sex written on it. People have somehow tried to persuade themselves that this is how it should be. Everything should be in a little box and the boxes should never be opened and spilt into each other. Some people collect so many boxes that they probably need a computer database to remember where all the boxes are. If you fall out with someone you put them in one of the little boxes, seal it shut and rarely move on from it. This stifles the grace of God.

For some people it is living one and a half, two or even more lives if it gets too complicated to manage. All of this may come from an erosion of truth – it is harder to understand what truth is these days, it is harder to see whether there is any truth left, 'surely everything is just opinions'. Also, the god of self comes into play.

We persuade ourselves that 'I am the most important person in the universe. Everything should revolve around me and that's why I can have all these boxes, and my life is not going to be challenged.' 'I like going to church with my friends, I like hanging out with people at festivals, but I don't really want it to spill over into the rest of my life, thank you very much.'

I have seen dualism in action, I have seen people at major Christian festivals falling over in the Spirit, praising God, really getting into it, being swept along with thousands of other young people and then trying to have sex with a stranger the same night and, amazingly, they don't seem to see that maybe there is a conflict between the two. I would have been racked by guilt about stuff like that yet they can somehow justify or ignore it – true dualism, like train tracks that never meet.

Being dualistic can be a sign of a bigger issue – do we actually know who God is and what he thinks of us? It can also be a sign of poor discipleship and hurts from the past not dealt with. I remember I kept my music away from God for many years. I thought that he would never be interested in it and it was only when I completely handed my music and my DJing over to God that he really started to use me and I found out that he loved hip hop, which was nice.

Fight!

Do we realise the battle that we are in when we are being dualistic? Do we know ourselves? Do we know our own heart? But I guess the real questions are: Do we really, really know God and his love for us? And, do we know the way he wants us to live our lives 24/7, with room for mistakes, not dividing life into separate little boxes and complicated ways of living which somehow justify our Christian existence?

Heart

Ultimately, the battleground is our heart. Believe that your heart is good and precious. We often simply think that we are bad people and are therefore cruel to ourselves, feeling that we are not worthy of God's unconditional love. Yet the Bible tells us that God loves us, he knew us before we were even born, and yet we still find that so difficult to handle. I think that is why so many people fall into dualism. It is somehow easier to put our lives in different little boxes than it is to accept that God really loves us unconditionally, including the nasty stuff that shocks even ourselves. 'Amazing grace, how sweet the sound that saved a wretch like me.'

Cheese

In the eighties there was a cheesy pop band called Bananarama. Most teenage boys at that time had fallen in love with them. They did a bad song which has been re-done recently: 'It's Not What You Do It's The Way That You Do It.' That is another big reason for dualism. In society today the media is full of cool-looking fashionable people with rarely very much talent and usually nothing to say. Radio 1 has excelled at this recently. I love a lot of the music the station plays, I still listen to it a bit, yet the DJs seem to have the ability to talk about nothing of any significance at all for 24 hours a day. It drives me mental. They spend their life DJing, talking about DJing and what they did last night while they were DJing – it goes round in circles, and is unbelievable at times.

Also, today some people are famous for being famous. That's quite impressive, to be famous for being famous. It's quite an easy way of making money! But who we are and what we do, is far more important than what we look like to others while doing it. Wrapped up in dualism, we can appear to be 'shiny' to certain people and look good to other people, but actually the way that we should live is in the open way that Jesus modelled. Remember that he lived in a community, where the houses were open or shared, there were extended families and probably no locks on the doors. There weren't very many places to hide away, unless you were a bored shepherd on a hillside. He lived his life in a very public and open way. We must strive for this kind of transparent lifestyle.

In Mt. 13, Jesus talks about the parable of the sower. The disciples were being really thick again and needed the whole thing explaining to them. Jesus said to them:

> Your ears are open but you don't hear a thing. Your eyes are awake but you don't see a thing. The people are blockheads! They stick their fingers in their ears so they won't have to listen; They screw their eyes shut so they won't have to look, so they won't have to deal with me face-to-face and let me heal them.

> (Mt. 13:14,15, The Message)

Jesus is saying, 'Look guys, don't live your life divided up into boxes, don't close your eyes to reality, don't play games with me, come to me, let's talk face to face,' and then a wonderful promise, 'let me heal them'. He is saying to us, if you face me then I will heal you. In verse 16 he continues, 'But you have God-blessed eyes – eyes that see! And God-blessed ears – ears that hear.' It would be great wouldn't it to have the balls to face God, face to face, and allow him to heal us from the insecurities that keep us locked up?

The statistics are definitely against us when it comes to integrity. According to a recent poll, 4 million husbands and wives across Britain have committed adultery. More than one in six married people told researchers they had been unfaithful to their current partner. For those who are in long-term relationships but unmarried it was one in five. And some people still think the figures for extra-marital affairs may be an underestimation, as it appears that women are less likely to admit to having an affair than men. And those from the affluent social classes are 50 per cent more likely to betray their partners than unskilled manual workers.

As I write this, I've just heard of a man I know who has had an affair and left his wife and young family. Our integrity is under attack, no doubt. Our first book, *Dead Men Walking*, was a call for genuine integrity not some weird patriarchal version of integrity that we have manufactured. Honesty and reality being the keys to genuine integrity and the ability to live your life in one big box. The ability to say to people 'read my mail', 'check my email', 'surf what I surf', 'park where I park', 'do what I do' is genuine freedom. As long as we don't allow it to disappear into legalism, it is genuine, genuine freedom. But we are not going to get there unless we have got one or two people that we can be honest with. It's that simple.

> Appoint leaders in every town according to my instructions. As you select them, ask, 'Is this man well-thought-of? Are his children believers? Do they respect him and stay out of trouble?' It's important that a church leader, responsible for the affairs in God's house, be looked up to – not pushy, not short-tempered, not a drunk, not a bully, not money-

hungry. He must welcome people, be helpful, wise, fair, reverent, have a good grip on himself, and have a good grip on the Message, knowing how to use the truth to either spur people on in knowledge or stop them in their tracks if they oppose it.

For there are a lot of rebels out there, full of loose, confusing, and deceiving talk. Those who were brought up religious and ought to know better are the worst. They've got to be shut up.

(Tit. 1:5–11, The Message)

I try to travel on the train as much as I can to save petrol and it gives me time to think. You start in the flashy new station, everything looks good, coffee and bagels are flowing, it's busy and looks businesslike, but as you pull out of the station you see the other side. You see the tracks that have been closed down, the sidings that are overgrown, the redundant buffers, and the old carriages that are rusting away. There is graffiti everywhere on the outbuildings. Then as you go into the countryside, you see scrapyards and the backs of people's houses. We often let everyone see the nice bits to our character but at some point we do need to let someone see the other parts of us as well – the parts of us that are not so nice, the thoughts we shouldn't be thinking, and the things we shouldn't be doing. If we don't deal with the darkness, we are simply not going to survive, like so many I have known. I have lived a semi-public life as a youth worker in Leeds for 11 years now and I realise that there is a pressure when people know and recognise you around the place. The easy way to deal with that is through genuine integrity, not to put your things in boxes, but to live a life which says, 'Yes, I do get frustrated with my kids in Morrisons but hey, it is still me!' Perfection isn't the goal, reality and therefore holiness is.

Oldies but goodies – tools for life

As a 35-year-old, it has been really helpful for me to learn from older people. There are a few older guys who I have a lot of respect for: Lawrie, Mike and of course my dad (who is wiser than he thinks!). There are others who I love to spend time with and understand. Lawrie gave us a few life tips in church a few weeks ago, like the importance of being honest about your feelings, but not becoming governed by them. If there is something wrong with us we need to get it fixed. If there is something that needs fixing in our heads, our bodies or spirits then we need to get it fixed. We ignore it at our peril.

Ravi Zaccharius, one of the most influential Christian apologists, says this, 'Give it to him or it will get you.' God cannot keep what you haven't given to him. 'Give it to him' – he repeats. In order to maintain integrity, we have to hand things over to God. And it is essential and helpful to actually speak that out in front of someone else.

> Make this your common practice: Confess your sins to each other and pray for each other so that you can live together whole and healed. The prayer of a person living right with God is something powerful to be reckoned with.
>
> (Jas. 5:16, The Message)

It is horrible doing it. I don't like to admit where I'm going wrong, I don't like to admit when I have argued with my wife, but I need to tell selected people those things. I have got a couple of guys that I can share stuff like that with and it makes an enormous difference. I know they will support me, I know they won't judge me and I know they will help me (or kick me!) through stuff.

The ritual of worship without some serious attempt at worthy living is a painted lie at best.

(George Butterick)

It is easier and simpler if we can just hand it over and say, 'Look God, I've messed up here please help me.' Or, 'Look God, I want to worship you now but I need to talk to you about this.' As we give the issue to him, it is exposed and loses its power over us and gets dealt with much quicker.

At Merseyfest (a mission event that mobilised the church in Liverpool in 2005), I had the real privilege of hearing George Verwer speak. George Verwer is one of the fathers of mission, and the founder of Operation Mobilisation. George had only 25 minutes to speak about mission to motivate the young people and amazingly he spent ten minutes talking about how he struggled in his youth with pornography. I was thinking, if he is booked to speak on mission what is he talking about pornography for? But for him I could see that, as he talked about these things openly, it was another way of him being accountable and honest, but also a way to speak to the lads there. He said, 'Look guys, it *will* destroy you, it can destroy you, it almost destroyed me, it will destroy you.' What a breath of fresh air! He was able to say 'get it out in the open', let's deal with it now so that we can get on with what God wants us to do. When someone at his age has been through all that stuff and served God for that length of time people like me need to listen. Thanks, George, for your honesty. I wish more leaders were as honest in public as you.

I can handle it!

For some of you reading this, you are thinking, 'Ah well, I do a few naughty things but it's not too bad. It's OK, I can handle it.' But if we take one or two steps on a slippery slope then we can easily fall down the mountainside and end up in a complete mess. Duffy Robbins talked about a real slippery slope in a mountain range in America. In this place, people think that they can ride downhill for part of it and then stop. But they realise that they can't stop and people have gotten seriously hurt or killed on this slope. Once you take the few steps that's it, you can't stop. If we are dabbling in stuff that we don't need to be involved in, we must not keep on doing it or it will get worse and we will go deeper *and* further. Give it to God now, talk about it with others and get it dealt with, plain and simple. It isn't rocket science!

Prov. 19:1 (CEV) says, 'It is better to be poor and live right than to be a stupid liar.' *The Message* says, 'Better to be poor and honest than a rich person no one can trust.'

Idi Amin, the infamous dictator of Uganda who died in 2003, was reported to be a complex character. He was responsible for up to 500,000 Ugandans dying directly from the orders that he had given, yet at the same time during his eight years in power, he seems to have had a reputation for being a practical joker. Bizarre.

In the Middle East, a Jewish settler broke into a mosque and opened fire with an assault rifle killing 29 Palestinian people. He was killed by the Palestinians around him after he had killed the people. His grave today is still a place of pilgrimage for many. On his gravestone it says, 'He was murdered for God, his hands are clean, he is a man of integrity.' These are both extreme examples, I know, but as Duffy Robbins said, it only took a slippery slope to get there.

As you know, we consider blessed those who have persevered. You have heard of Job's perseverance and have seen what the Lord finally brought about. The Lord is full of compassion and mercy.

Above all, my brothers, do not swear – not by heaven or by earth or by anything else. Let your 'Yes' be yes, and your 'No', no, or you will be condemned.

Is any one of you in trouble? He should pray. Is anyone happy? Let him sing songs of praise.

(Jas. 5:11–13, NIV)

You see God makes it very clear – pray if we are in trouble, sing God's praises when we are doing well, let our 'yes be yes', our 'no be no'. Just for a minute think of all the difficult situations you have been in. How much easier would everything have been if you'd simply applied those principles?

We make Christianity a weird and scary thing when, actually, sometimes it is really simple. We need to get on and live out the faith that God has given us in a way that our light will shine, rather than being dull and blurry.

Questions to chew on

- Discuss the word integrity – what does it mean to you?
- What does Titus 1 have to say to us today?
- Name someone you think has integrity.
- Have you ever been let down when someone has disappointed you in life?
- What 'boxes' do you have to deal with?
- Jas. 5:16 – have you ever done that?
- Let your partner write a piece on you and share it with others!

- Discuss how you think God deals with your character not your gifts.
- Watch the film *The Apostle* and then discuss it in the light of this chapter.

Note

1   *Saved*, United Artists Films Inc., 2004.

Thou shalt not buy a car in the colours of brown, pink, lime-green, orange or sky blue.

19

Individuality

MATT PAGE

We live in a culture where our individuality matters. There are hundreds of opportunities to show how we are different to everyone else through the clothes we wear, the way we decorate our house, the music we listen to and so on. Yet when it comes to changing the world, for good or for bad, all of a sudden we think we are insignificant, that our contribution to the whole doesn't matter.

This summer at a Christian festival, I sat for an hour or so near a low hedge and watched as various groups of people climbed over it so they didn't have to walk for an extra 30 seconds. Over that hour, the hedge got gradually more and more damaged and broken. I suspect that if you had asked any of those concerned what they would think about a bunch of Christians destroying a hedge they would have thought it was appalling. Yet actually each one of them contributed to its damage because they didn't consider their role significant.

That's a trivial example. But scale it up a bit and you have a world of huge injustice undergoing massive environmental destruction. The inhabitants of the planet look on in horror at what is happening, but shrugging their shoulders as to what they can do – they are just one person.

I also wondered during the LIVE 8 concerts whether all those who went would acknowledge their individual responsibility to live in a way that was in line with the issues they had been protesting about. How many see it as something for their government alone to sort out, shrugging their individual responsibility to pay a bit more for clothes that weren't made in a sweatshop, or to eat food where the workers were paid a fair wage?

The fact is, we *are* significant. We are children of the living God. Every action we take echoes through eternity. On the one hand, it could be the careless discarding of an apple core, the unnecessary journey in the car. On the other hand, it could be buying a fairly-traded product even though it is more expensive, or witnessing to one single person in a lost world. But if we live like our choices don't matter then we devalue the worth and significance God has placed on us. There is an enemy who wants us to shrink from our significance, and wants us all to believe that even if we do the right thing, no one else will. The problem is that so many of us believe it! Imagine if we all believed that we are significant and we can make a difference. We actually would! Why not start now?

First, we are called to right living not just doing the things that work, and avoiding the things that are really bad. Right living doesn't always bring the right results, but it can still be right. And the right choices we make, however futile we consider their impact to be, can still make a difference.

Secondly, our culture is obsessed with lone heroes. Often there is a group of people all working hard to achieve something. But the media wants to give us lone heroes so it overlooks most of the team and transforms one member of it into the sole hero. Would we even have heard of Mother Teresa unless hundreds of nuns had also taken vows of poverty and served to help the poor? Don't believe it. We won't all be the leader who is solely responsible for changing the world. But those changes we desire will be taken step by step, and by people pulling in the same direction to achieve things.

Finally, how we live can make a difference to individuals that should not be overlooked. My switching to fairly-traded chocolate may not end world poverty on its own, but it might be enough to lift a family out of poverty. My sharing the gospel might not transform my whole town, but it may bring someone into a life-changing relationship with God.

We are not insignificant.

We are made in the image of the almighty God, and equipped by his Spirit. Let's get out there and live like every single thing we do changes the world in one way or another. It does.

For groups and you ...

- What makes us significant?
- Do you really believe that your life counts?
- How does our view of ourselves affect the way we treat the environment?
- When was the last time you felt significant? What made you feel that way?
- What changes do you have to make in attitude and behaviour if you are the son or daughter of God?

www.openheaven.org

Christian leadership often consists of re-structuring, re-configuring, re-naming and re-branding. Anything that looks like something is happening but doesn't rock the boat, nor enable it to leave the shore.

(Paul Sinclair)

20

Over the Wall

LEE SAVILLE

I have always been a pretty focused individual. At the age of 11, I decided that I wanted to be a solicitor. And that was it: that was my focus. Once old enough, I qualified and loved it straight away. It drew me in and wrapped around me, a perfect fit. I became a workaholic, then a partner and eventually managing partner. I grew to love titles. I became Secretary of the local Law Society, a local part-time lecturer and then a 'non-Council member of the Property and Commercial Services Committee of the Law Society' (a big title that one). The law gave me money, respect, position. It seemed to feed everything in me that needed feeding. What I didn't see then was how it consumed me at the same time.

I married, and subsequently divorced, spending far too many hours at my desk. When my wife left me, I dug deeper into my work. My work was always pleased to see me, it always rewarded me, it was always there.

I filled my life with all the things that you would expect from a wealthy single man. I bought a large house and employed a housekeeper to look after both it and me. I bought a Golf GTI (when they were still considered quick), and an Alpha Romeo Spider as a second soft-top sunny day car. I filled my house with antique furniture and every modern device known to man.

On Saturdays, I would often stagger back to the car under the weight of boxes and bags of things I felt I couldn't live without. I would fill the tiny boot of the Spider, go home, and swap cars to party for the evening. Then do the same thing the following weekend, arriving again at the boot of the car only to discover as I opened it, that my precious purchases from the week before were still there.

Was I happy? I thought so. Everyone told me I should be.

I didn't know any Christians. My view was they were weak, naïve, dull, boring people who needed a crutch to get themselves through their lives. People who probably needed a shrink but couldn't afford one, so joined small groups to work out their problems.

Christians broke into my world in around 1984. A young guy called Jeremy arrived in my office to work as a trainee solicitor. On his first day, I found him over lunch reading his Bible. I had never seen anyone do that before: it shocked me.

He invited me for dinner, lasagne. He and his friends wolfed it down quickly and then stood up telling me they were going to a baptism, did I want to come?

I smiled inside. 'They think they've trapped me,' I thought. But I was a party animal, a drinker of wine, a gambler, a driver of fast cars, a lawyer, a man with ambition, and his boss! 'They have no idea who they are dealing with!' I thought. (I am sure God must have smiled.)

Snow falling, we walked to a small old church where the heating didn't work. We took seats towards the back. I realised that I would be in for more than I had bargained for when the woman who came to sit beside me took her own tambourine out of a polythene bag!

After what seemed an endless time of people waving their arms in the air and singing songs and, so far as the woman beside me was concerned, banging her tambourine, everyone was invited to move towards the front to watch the baptism. The guy at the front encouraged visitors to find a good spot so that they could see everything. At the time, it all seemed choreographed to me. A passage opened up through the crowd of hand-clappers, who half turned, extending their arms towards me, like a scene from 'the living dead' encouraging me to get closer and closer to the front.

There in the floor was a tank of water. Tiles cracked and discoloured. Steam rising into the very cold air. A big guy dressed in white stood at the microphone and through tears began to confess things that, had I been his lawyer, I would have advised him to keep to himself. His openness made me feel uncomfortable and embarrassed for him. Then he climbed into the pale green water and two men lowered him backwards until he was completely immersed. As he came out of the water I remember thinking to myself, 'What on earth would make someone do a thing like that?!'

Sometime later, Jeremy invited me to what he told me was a kind of talk on healing. It turned out to be an evening meeting at a John Wimber conference. People cried and laughed – I sat down, not really sure what to think.

I will never forget Jeremy. His faith, his absolute conviction, his zeal and his courage in the face of all of my cynicism. He moved to another job and I lost contact with him until quite recently.

Nine years passed before Christians again came my way. Anyone who thinks that the mission field is in a foreign land should ponder on that. I met Tim through some friends at a party and he mentioned that he went to the church I had visited with Jeremy years earlier.

(I struggled to force images of the woman with the tambourine out of my mind.) He introduced me to his pastor, Mike. A bright eyed, intelligent man who I immediately liked and became friends with. It was Mike who persuaded me to run the various gauntlets of 'nurture group' (even the name still makes me cringe) and later Alpha. (All of which I kept secret from my family, my work colleagues and my girlfriend.) He even persuaded me to try church.

After six months of church, it seemed to me like any other club. Meetings, activities, rule books. I decided it was not for me and went to what I thought would be my last Sunday. It was in that meeting that God touched me. I cried for over an hour. The young guy who was praying with me asked if I knew what had happened. I remember thinking, 'Yes, I have just had a nervous breakdown. All those people who said you have been working too hard, maybe they were right, Lee.'

As I drove home that afternoon, still shaken by what had happened, an unrelated thought dropped into my head, 'Get Mike to go to Toronto.' (It was the early summer of 1994, I had heard nothing of what God had begun to do in a little church by the airport runway in Toronto, and so this made no sense to me.) It came over and over again. I was now sure that I needed time off work! For just over one week, this thought would not leave me alone. It kept coming into my mind when I was driving to work, as I sat at my desk holding on for someone to answer the phone, or whenever my mind began to drift. Each night that week I woke up at about 2:45 a.m., 'Get Mike to go to Toronto.' I felt that if I could just tell Mike what was going round in my head then it might stop and I might get some sleep. But it sounded crazy, even to me, and if I was on the edge of a nervous breakdown it was not something that I really wanted to publicise.

One week later, at my wits' end, I plucked up the courage.

'Mike, have you ever thought about going to Toronto?' It sounded stupid and lame.

'Why do you say that?' he asked.

I stumbled over my words and tried to explain as best I could. I felt foolish. Even as I was explaining to him I felt as though I was suggesting he go to the far ends of the earth without any proper logical or justifiable explanation. Then I heard myself say, 'And if no one will go with you, I will go!'

'Why did you say that?' I thought.

Anyhow, I had told him, and hopefully now I could get on with my life.

Some days later, Mike said he would go to Toronto and so (out of a sense of obligation) I found myself sitting in Heathrow airport with Charlie (who had led the Alpha course) and Mike, all three clutching tickets to Toronto. I suspect that both Charlie and Mike thought that I knew why and where we were going. I had no idea.

The Toronto Airport Vineyard church turned out to be a small industrial unit by the airport. We were given the last seats in the second row from the front. There were some women sitting immediately in front of us, and the one directly in front of me clearly had a problem. She simply did not seem to be able to keep her arms still. They would fly up into the air above her head, and as she seemed to get them back under control, off they would go again. Every so often, her head would begin to shake from side to side and then off her hands would go again. She was sitting so close to me that I couldn't ignore her, and eventually she began to irritate me a little.

Then the meeting began. The worship was great. I was not very experienced in such things and I was not really into music and so had only been to a few concerts in my life, but it was simply great. But the women in front of me gave me cause for concern. The woman with the arms seemed to find a new lease of life as the worship team began, her arms now dancing in the air above her head. The woman beside her was dancing what seemed to be silly little steps. I tried not to look at them, but it wasn't easy.

Then the worship leader asked for people to give testimony. A solid young guy got up onto the platform, and as he did I noticed that he was twitching. He told us that he and his girlfriend had come to Toronto to try to find God again. As he spoke he stammered and the people in the room laughed at him. He told us that after one night in the meeting they realised that they had put God in a box. And so he said, 'We moved God to another box.' After two nights they 'moved God to a bigger box' and after last night he said, 'We ain't got a box big enough!' And with that, he fell over and landed on the ground just in front of the row of waving women. I now looked at the room around me with different eyes. I could not believe that I travelled all this way to come to this. This was the very worst of everything I had ever heard about American Christian television evangelism. The preacher gave a simple message, but my eyes did not leave the young guy lying on the floor, who I had already condemned as a fool or a fraud in my mind. His whole body shook all the way through the message. At the time it never occurred to me that it would be just about impossible to do this voluntarily, and certainly not for a whole 40 minutes. By the end of the message he was covered in sweat and still vibrating. I wanted to go home, I was tired, and my cynical analytical lawyer's mind would not be still.

The preacher then said that they wanted to pray for people and that we should clear the chairs to the side of the room. There were a few moments of organised chaos as chairs were stacked and cleared away. The waving women turned and faced the body of the hall.

As the ministry team prayed for people, those prayed for fell to the ground. I had never seen anything like this. I concluded I was witnessing the results of mass hysteria or hypnosis. A woman directly in front of me fell backwards towards me and involuntarily I caught her and lowered her to the ground. The woman who was praying for her smiled at me (it was the waving woman) her finger hovered in the air level with her face, waving gently from left to right as if it was held there by a breeze and as the woman slowly got on her knees to continue praying she gently said to me, 'You next.'

I began to clutch for straws. I was a drinker, a party animal, a lover of speed and fun. However misguided they might have been, these were after all only Christians, so what did I have to fear? I had travelled this far, I might as well have my turn.

I prayed. I had read and heard about God, I so much wanted him to be real, 'If this is really you, Lord, I want all that you have for me, and if it's not you I don't want any of it. But if it really is you, Lord, then you are going to have to knock me off my feet, because I don't care if I am the last man standing, I am not going to fall over to make these people happy.'

She began to pray and to my great surprise I fell backwards. I quickly struggled to regain control. She stepped over me, smiling, and moved on.

As I sat and looked around I felt in my heart as if something had come very close to me and I had pulled away from it. It was not something that I thought in my head, it was something that I felt in my heart and the feeling grew and grew. I sat on the floor and closed my eyes. I felt someone come and sit beside me. I felt sure it was Mike. I could feel his knee against my knee. I could feel the heat of his shoulder and arm against my shoulder and arm. My mind began to race for something smart to say. Something that wouldn't make me appear too vulnerable. I opened my eyes as I began to say, 'This is a wacky church, Mike!' and to my amazement found there was no one there. I was shocked. I would have bet everything I owned that there was someone crowding my space. And as my head was still reeling with this, I heard what was by then becoming a familiar voice in my head say, 'It's OK, Lee, I'm here when you're ready.' I burst into tears.

The next night, I met him, my Lord, my God. My life has never been the same since. I still don't know how you ever prepare anyone for that, for the reality of a living God.

What can you say when God touches you? I was baptised the next weekend in that same little church I had visited with Jeremy for the first time in 1984. For the next year and a half, I felt that life could not get any better. Everything that had seemed important to me faded in the light of him. He became my focus and all I wanted to do was run after him.

My mum and dad became Christians, one of my friends at work and his family became Christians. I still had my big house, two cars, big income and housekeeper, but now I also had Jesus in my life. It was great.

Then, one year later, in the summer of 1995 I began to have visions. At first eyes closed, then eyes open. They were always the same. An open field. Ankle deep, broad blade grass. The back of the field covered with smoke or fog. I was standing behind a dry-stone wall. Then suddenly a little boy burst out of the fog, eyes wide, terrified, mouth open screaming, never any sound. Face dirty, hair matted, clothes dirty and torn, no shoes, running as fast as he could to get to the wall. It was safe on my side of the wall.

Then another child, dirty face, torn clothes, no shoes, running as fast as he could, screaming, trying to get to the wall. Then a young girl. She held the hand of a young child (her son) aged about three or four years old. Dirty, torn clothes, no shoes, running for the wall.

Something was chasing them. Something I never saw. Her hand slipped. She let go of the child. She didn't want to, she didn't mean to. She was so scared, running so fast. And each time I saw this, as she let go of his hand, it was as if a huge wave hit me in the chest and I would just erupt in tears.

Then his voice, 'Go over the wall Lee.'

Up and over the wall and into the field, like watching it on TV, I ran to the first child and picked him up and ran back towards the wall and put him over it. Then back into the field to the next child and the next one and the next one and on and on it would go.

Refugees I thought; 'Street children,' God said.

I figured I would go to Brazil. I knew there were street children there. I would find a project working with street kids, go for two weeks, find out what I could and then come home and make money and send it. But whilst I was making my plans, God was unfolding his.

Some people in my church had begun to make plans to visit a church in Arad, Romania, to run a conference on the Holy Spirit, and at the last minute they asked me to join the prayer team. I knew nothing about Romania. If you had shown me a map of Europe I would not have known where Romania was. I did not know it had come through a revolution, I had not heard about its poverty and its problems. I had heard years earlier about its orphanages, but that had been a long time ago. I had not heard about Romania's street children.

On my first full day in Romania, I climbed out of a taxi and came face to face with the children I had spent the previous six months watching in visions running towards the dry-stone wall. I was stunned, I felt ambushed. I felt that if God was going to do this then surely he would have talked to me about it. He wouldn't have just presented me with this.

As I approached them, my mind was racing, full of my own anxieties. How would I react to them? How would they react to me? What about lice and fleas and disease? A list of concerns scrolled through my mind. And then as I took those last steps, it was as if my heart was opened and a love poured into me that I knew was not mine and all of my doubts and anxieties melted away. Even more amazing to me was that I could see on the faces of these children and young people that they could feel this love, too.

Each day I met up with Laura (the daughter of the pastor of the church we were visiting), and went to the street to meet up with these children. At the end of the week, I extended my air ticket another week trying to get my head around what was going on. And at the end of two weeks, the truth is that I knew what God wanted me to do, but I didn't want to do it. Even thinking about doing it would make my heart beat hard.

What would my friends say? I had worked so hard to become a lawyer, to gain position and wealth. It would be mad to give it up.

I flew home trying to put some distance between me and the emotional situation in which I found myself. I needed to find someone who could speak some wisdom into me. By which I meant, someone who could talk me out of this.

For one week, I struggled in the UK, unable to eat or sleep properly. I tried to do a deal with God. 'I will go for three months. I will find out all that I can about street children and then I will come home and make money and send it.' And so I went.

Every day we would go to the street, carrying home-made soup in margarine cartons, and every day I would feel the love of God come. For the first few months, I spent a lot of time in tears. I would sit and look at these children, hurt, abandoned, hungry, scared, full of parasites, living in holes in the ground, children looking after children, and I would weep. Often some little kid, dirty faced and full of lice, would come up and sit by the side of me, confused about why I was crying and would put his arm around me and say, 'Don't cry, Lee.' At night as I sat in my room, my head would click in. My logical analytical head. 'This makes no sense. What about my home, my career, my life?' I had worked so hard to get to where I was, I had made so many sacrifices. What about my mum and dad?

Each day this battle would go on, my heart would fill with the love of God and each night my head would click in.

By the end of my three months, it was not that God had said anything new to me. It was not that I had received new revelation. He had told me what he wanted me to do right at the beginning, and I had been fighting him, and after three months, I simply could not fight him any longer.

I went home and resigned from my partnership, sold my cars and rented out my home (and later sold it) and moved back to Arad to work full-time with street children and the poorest of the poor. Most of my friends thought I was nuts.

It was then, after I moved back to Arad, that I saw God begin to move in a new way.

We looked for a room to move the feeding programme to. No one would rent us anything when they knew what we wanted it for. Then God led us to a house. A small mud brick building in a village 7 km away from the city. I remember standing and looking at it and feeling it was too small and in too poor a condition for our use. But when we got inside, it was full of the presence of God. The owner wanted 23,000 DM, which was too much. But God's hand was so clearly on it. The vendor said he would wait three months for us to raise the cash and I left that day making my plans. (It took me a long time to learn that my plans never work as well as God's.) My plan was to write to everyone I knew. Surely, we could raise 23,000 DM (about £7,000)? A whole week went by and I had no time to write to anyone. Every day spent on the street, and every night in the hospital with kids trying to get them treatment. I remember feeling guilty on the Friday night. A whole week had gone by and I had not done anything to communicate this need. Then on the Saturday evening I received a phone call from a man I didn't know and had never heard of, from a city I had never been to. He said, 'Hello, my name is Ingemar. I am calling you from Gothenborg in Sweden. The Lord has spoken to me and I have to come to see you.'

I was tired and when I'm tired I get a bit impatient (I'm working on it). I said if he came to Arad he should ask any child on the street where to find me and they would tell him and then I ended the conversation. Looking back it seems odd even to me. I didn't take a number or address. I just hung up and didn't think about him again. After a few days, he turned up at the feeding programme. He stood at a distance and waited until we had finished and then said, 'Hi, I'm Ingemar, I spoke to you on the telephone. The Lord has sent me and I have to speak to you.' We went for coffee and he asked me to tell him everything that we were doing at that time. I told him about children living in holes in the ground and the horror of street life and then at the end almost as an afterthought I said, 'Oh and we feel the Lord has led us to a building and we are about to start trying to raise money to buy it.' His face lit up. A big smile. He asked, 'How much is the building?'

'23,000 DM,' I replied.

He touched his bag and said, 'I have exactly 23,000 DM here. The Lord told me to bring it, I didn't know why. Now I do.'

Since then I have seen God work in similar ways over and over again.

I have found myself travelling a roller coaster from peaks of faith into troughs of doubt.

The lawyer in me is forever wanting to plan and to drive. My nature is to dot 'i's and cross 't's but I have learned that some of the things that interest me don't seem to be of much interest to God. Often, as we have been struggling to finish the last thing that he began, he will announce prophetically the next thing he is going to do, and our prayer many times is, 'Please don't do that yet.' Rarely does he seem to listen to these prayers and suddenly the next thing is breathed into being and we find ourselves running to try to manage that, too.

It always feels as if we have too few people or too few of the right skills. It always feels as though we don't have quite enough resources to reach as far as he is taking us, but he always gets it just right.

Since 1996 I have watched as he provided homes and a day centre for the homeless, food and bread for the hungry and wood to heat the homes of the poor (−25°C and below in the winter here). I have watched as he has begun things in the right season and brought them to an end as a season has ended. I have watched over and over again as he has called the right people at the right time. He has always been faithful. Always providing for our needs (which I have discovered are sometimes very different from our 'wants'). And although it has been a tough lesson for me, I have learned to trust him.

Since 1996 my family has been made up of my mum and dad (who still live in Sheffield and who I miss a lot) and children and young people who have lived on the streets, in some cases for over 15 years. In the last nine years, they have laughed and cried with me, and shared in both joy, and sorrow and pain.

He told us clearly that he was raising up people from amongst the street children and poor to minister to those around them. Years passed and I began to lose hope of this happening but then after nearly ten years we have begun to see some of the young people who have grown up with us give their lives to the Lord and develop such a hunger and passion for him it is awesome to watch.

Now they are beginning to reach out into the poor communities around us. Helping kids in families like the ones they ran away from. Helping us to help the very poor. They are not afraid of poverty or dirt or parasites. They are not afraid of disease. They know what it is to be cold and hungry and alone. They are not afraid of sharing their faith and sometimes when I stand and watch them I think of Jeremy.

Questions

- Are you the only Christian some of the people you work with get to meet?
- What boxes do you put God into?
- Do the opinions of people stop you from stepping into the things God asks you to do?
- What are the things that you want to hold on to (e.g. reputation, position, money, stuff) that stop you grabbing God with both hands?

www.networks.org.ro

If the world should blow itself up, the last audible voice would be that of an expert saying 'It can't be done.'

(Peter Ustinov)

21

Fine

BAZ GASCOYNE

One of the things I hate about church more than anything else is the lack of honesty that can often be seen. In every Sunday and mid-week meeting, people are welcomed and asked the same thing, 'How are you?' Every week the same answer is given, 'Fine thank you, and you?' 'Oh fine.'

If the truth was really spoken, the person who is fine may well say, 'Actually I'm not fine', and inform the enquirer of the struggles they are experiencing. But the fear in all of us is that this would be received with a horrified look of, 'I don't really want to know what is going on in your life, I was just being polite.'

Well, I am on a mission to ban the word 'fine' in the church today. Why? Because the gospel (the good news of Jesus) is not for 'fine' people. It's for people who are broken, helpless, who are in pain physically and emotionally. It's for the lonely, depressed, angry, bitter, the struggling, people with addictions and fears without hope or a purpose. It's for people carrying unforgiveness in their lives and who are bogged down with their sin. It's for the bereaved, misunderstood, the wealthy and the poor. Whatever condition the person's life, heart and mind is in, this is who Jesus is for and not a *fine* brigade.

Billy Graham once said, 'I've listened to too many sermons and seen too many Christian films with happy-ever-after endings. Becoming a Christian isn't the end of your problems, it's the beginning of you facing up to them' (*Get Real*, Mal Fletcher, Word Books, 1993).

I think of a gentleman I met at a recent church gathering who always seemed very cheerful and fine when you asked him, but who recently committed suicide. Obviously, he wasn't as fine as he appeared. We need to create an environment where people can come with all their crap and be accepted and loved to such an extent that will encourage them to open up and begin to let God into the areas that need healing and forgiveness.

There is the well-known saying: 'People need to feel they belong before they believe and before they behave.' But for too long the church has said: 'You need to believe and behave before you belong.'

We need to create environments where it's OK to be honest; where leaders are leading by example and showing that it's OK to be vulnerable.

Someone recently gave me a great acronym for the world FINE: Feelings Inside Not Expressed. Most guys are desperate to be able to say how they really feel without feeling that they are going to be looked down upon or written off. Well, gentlemen, I have felt 'fine' many times and I'm sure I will in the future and no one is going to stop me from admitting it because they want nice comfortable meetings. 'Nice, comfortable meetings' never change a thing but a 'God meeting' certainly does. I keep saying to the church that if we have a hat-trick of 'just good meetings' we should close the church as the only thing that makes a difference is a 'God meeting'.

I want to encourage you to take a risk and express what is really going on in your life with someone you know, trust and love and begin the process of unravelling all that baggage squashed inside that is bursting to get out.

> People are never more insecure than when they become obsessed with their fears at the expense of their dreams.
>
> (Norman Cousins)

Why should you and I be robbed of our dreams and the dreams God has for us because we are obsessed with our fears? Being honest robs of those fears of their power.

So if someone asks you, 'How are you?' why not answer truthfully, be it 'Fantastic' or 'Terrible actually'. Or if you ask someone else and they answer, 'Fine,' why not ask them what that really means?

What I like about so many characters in the Bible is that they were transparent with what was really going on in their lives. So we have men who were warriors, full of passion and strength, but also men with weaknesses. Abraham was known as a friend of God but he was also a liar. David messed up but then owned up to it as soon as he was confronted. The mighty Paul would happily let people know about his past and his feelings of unworthiness: he was not afraid to be himself and for others to see this. Look at 1 Cor. 15:19; Eph. 3:8; 1 Tim. 1:15.

We need a greater freedom among the men in the church so that we model what is so evident in the Bible: WYSIWYG (What You See Is What You Get). Hey, maybe I could put that on a rubber wristband and make my fortune!

So let's take a risk and build relationships that are real. Are you wearing a mask afraid to be yourself? Are you angry, bitter, hurting, even contemplating suicide but wondering if you can really be yourself and tell someone? Well, the answer is yes. How do I know this? Because I have allowed, and still am allowing, the real Baz to be seen and people are still here and have not dumped me. I am discovering who I should be and who God wants me to be.

Philip Yancey says, 'There is nothing I can do to make God love me more and there is nothing I can do to make God love me less.' Why not take a risk and see that it is true. Stop being 'fine' and be you, because that's who God intended you to be. All God asks is for me to be the best Baz Gascoyne I can be. All he asks of you is to be the best whatever your name is.

'A man who is fine will not achieve anything or feel fulfilled as a man; a man who is real, transparent and vulnerable will become a Man. The Man God intended him to be.'

Questions

- Do you feel FINE today?
- What feelings inside have you never expressed?
- Will you take a risk today and be honest with a mate about what is really going on in your life?
- Do you want to know the freedom that Jesus offers you today?

I usually make up my mind about a man in 10 seconds and I very rarely change it.

(Margaret Thatcher)

22

Autopilot

LEE JACKSON

I was in Leeds city centre, I had to buy some stuff for the youth event that I was doing. It was lunchtime so I grabbed a sandwich and a can of Coke while walking down Albion Street. I had a bag full of DVDs and prizes for this youth event, was balancing my drink and enjoying the hussle of the city centre. Then I saw a police van pull up in front of me and out of the back of the van jumped three policewomen, two of them went straight over to have a word with someone who was next to the bank on my left. This guy had a rucksack on his back and it was fair to say that he looked a little bit shifty. I was about 50 yards away when they asked to have a look in his rucksack. He took the bag off his back, then all of a sudden, started running. He pushed past the police and leapt over a pushchair, knocking the child over. The child's mum, obviously shocked, started to go a bit mad. He stumbled towards me trying to get away and without thinking I punched him on his back, pushed him to the ground and sat on him. I dropped my shopping and I kept my knees in his back as the police handcuffed him. They were obviously shaken by this incident as well and they put him in the back of the van. It was over in only a few seconds. The odd thing about it was that the police officers never acknowledged me or said anything to me, they just put him in the back of the van and then they drove off. I was frozen in the middle of town, my Coke had flown in the air, my shopping was all over the floor and I just stood there dazed, as the mum picked up the child in the pushchair (who was OK) and walked away. I was stood in this daze in the street suddenly realising what I had just done. I genuinely didn't think about it, it was just something that happened and I was 'on autopilot' at the time.

As I went and finished off the rest of my shopping in town, walking round in a daze, not quite understanding what I had just done, my mind raced with the implications of what could have happened … what if he had needles in his pocket? What if he was armed? A bizarre moment in my life! But being a youth worker and a speaker you think about times like these and how it affects you. It really got me thinking about how much we actually do 'on autopilot'. How much of our faith, and even our life is done on autopilot? Also, how much of our life is deliberate …

> A car salesman, bruised and battered as he was dragged along the road trying to foil carjackers, today vowed: 'I would do the same again.' Brave Christian Lawson, aged 22, was carried for around 300 yards on the outside of a Ford Focus as he tried to stop criminals accelerating away. As the car gathered speed, he tried to launch himself towards a grass verge, but failed and ended up striking the carriageway in East Bank Road, Arbourthorne. He sustained a gash to his eyebrow which needed five stitches and bruises and grazing to the rest of his body. But today Christian, who lives on the Manor estate, said, 'A lot of people have said I should have just let them take the car, but I would probably do it again. There wasn't any time to think.' Christian, who works for Dixon Ford, had no reason to suspect

the two men involved were anything other than legitimate customers and offered a test drive in the Ford. He took the wheel initially and the men struck as he swapped places to allow one of them to drive the car. They attacked him as he got into the passenger seat, taking the ignition keys, thumping him and then pushing him out of the vehicle. The offenders then set off.

(http://www.sheffieldtoday.net/ViewArticle2.aspx ?SectionID=58&ArticleID=826065, 21 July 2004)

I'm not sure whether Christian Lawson did think about what he was doing at the time, but he did say that he would do it again. Putting his life at risk to save a piece of metal. When you think about being on autopilot, I guess the question you ask is what have I done while being on autopilot?

Why not stop now and think about the incidents that have happened to you? Times when you have reacted naturally, without a chance to think, times when you may have been threatened, at risk or even your family and friends were in danger, an accident that you might have seen, a story personal to you. Let it sink in for a few minutes ...

So, is this our most natural state or is it our false state of being? Doing things instinctively rather than pre-planned or pre-meditated?

Well, it's not the men in your life that counts, it's the life in your men.

(Mae West's character 'Tira', from the 1933 Paramount film *I'm No Angel*)

So many things that we do in church and our Christian life can be seen as pre-meditated, even as manipulative. Speakers use emotional stories, and certain worship songs draw on our emotions and God uses all of that but sometimes you know you are actually being manipulated. Some people would say that what you do on autopilot is 'the real you'. It's the genuine response that you give. It has been said that if you have a meal with someone and they are nice to you but nasty to the waiter, then they are genuinely not a good person because their interaction with the waiter shows their real self. When you are shocked or when someone cuts you up in the car, what is your reaction?

Smith

As I thought through this autopilot thing some more, I started thinking about one of my heroes, Smith Wigglesworth. I started to think about his life and some of the amazing stories that are told about him. Did he act on autopilot or not? Living in the north of England, Smith Wigglesworth somehow seems more real to me. At Bridge Street Church in Leeds, where my friend Andy is the youth pastor, the church's foundation stone was laid in November 1930 by George Jeffries, the famous revivalist. There is a photograph in the church of him laying the stone, and we wonder whether the guy standing next to him is actually Smith Wigglesworth. They were good friends and you'd think that as George Jeffries had travelled up from London that maybe he did see Smith while he was nearby. It is very possible that when the foundation stone was laid, at one of the oldest and most influential churches in Leeds, Smith Wigglesworth was there.

Yorkshire lad

Smith was born in 1859 in Burley in Wharfedale, which is on the outskirts of Leeds. He was confirmed at All Saints Church in Otley, the town where one of my friends,

Claire, works. And he moved to Bradford at age 13. He was an uneducated Yorkshire man, he couldn't read or write very much, but he became a plumber and was obviously very good with his hands. He was a practical, down-to-earth Yorkshire guy. A biographer said that he had a gruff voice and he had a stammer. Even in later life as he got over the problem with the stammer, he was definitely an 'unpolished speaker': you weren't going to get lots of nice stories with seven points, the first letter of each making an acronym, with Smith! He didn't mess about, he just went for it. He wasn't eloquent but God used him enormously. He was a stocky man, medium height and physically fit, a very keen cricketer. He was particularly well groomed – in all the photographs that you see of him he looks very smart. Even though he didn't have much money, he was always 'turned out well' and made a lot of effort in his appearance. One of the amazing things about Smith is that even in all his roughness and with his unpolished background, he was a very compassionate man. He was often seen weeping over a child who was ill and was brought to him. He was often seen weeping as he prayed for people. We see him as an upright Yorkshire man, straight talking, yet at the same time compassionate. His heart broke when he saw illness. He was a living paradox, a well-groomed but rough exterior, an uneducated man, yet one of the most influential Christian leaders we have ever had. A working class plumber whose heart broke when he saw a child that was ill.

A hero is one who does what he can. The others don't.

(Romain Rolland)

One of my favourite stories about Smith is local to me here in Yorkshire. O. G. Miles – a pastor and great friend of

Wigglesworth – relates a remarkable incident illustrating the leading of the Holy Spirit in Wigglesworth's life.

> One day, Wigglesworth and James Salter visited Miles at his home in Leeds. Suddenly, Wigglesworth said to the two men, 'God is telling me to go to Ilkley Moor', he was speaking of a lovely town frequented by tourists about 16 miles away from Leeds city centre. Because of the war, petrol was rationed but Miles said he would have to drive them. When they arrived they stopped at a lovely spot known as the Cow and Calf rocks, no soul was in sight so they seated themselves on an overlook. For some time, nothing happened causing Miles and Salter to think that Wigglesworth must have been mistaken, however, Wigglesworth had no misgivings and he was soon proven correct. A young man with a pack on his back appeared and sat down for rest next to Wigglesworth, soon the two were talking. The young man was a backslider who, like the prodigal, was disillusioned with sin. In a few moments there on the moor the man knelt with Wigglesworth and came back to God. 'What a prayer meeting we had that day on Ilkley Moor,' Miles later said. Then suddenly as before, Wigglesworth said, 'George you can take me back now I have done what God has told me to do.'
>
> How this man was in touch with heaven waiting for words from the throne for anything God wanted him to do! And the Lord certainly knew who to send on such an important mission, his faithful and trusted friend – Smith Wigglesworth.
>
> (Albert Hibbert, *Smith Wigglesworth: The Secret of His Power*, Tulsa: Harrison House Publishers, 1993. Used with kind permission.)

Smith Wigglesworth was one of a long line of what Americans like to call 'rrrrevivalists'. Others are Evan

Roberts from the Welsh revival, where an estimated 100,000 people came to know God, George Jeffries and his brothers, and Duncan Campbell from the Hebridian revival.

> A hero is no braver than an ordinary man, but he is braver five minutes longer.
>
> (Ralph Waldo Emerson – US essayist and poet (1803–82))

So, living in Leeds and reading stories like Smith's, I wonder what similarities there were between him and us, how he lived and whether he made 'God choices'. The more I read about Smith Wigglesworth, I realise that although there was an aspect of being 'on autopilot' with him, there is no doubt about that, it still appears that he made choices all the time. Choices to live in the way that he did, choices to step out, choices to not be afraid to upset the status quo of church life. And amazingly, it always appeared that he was in the right place at the right time. He spent so much time talking to God that he always seemed to know what God wanted him to do at that moment. In Hibbert's book, he writes that the success of Wigglesworth's ministry was not caused by his ability but rather by his availability. I just wonder sometimes how available we are for God, when we are tied up with the things that crowd our lives, and the priorities that we give to things that need no priority. It is important that we ask God to help us on the inside, to change us from the inside, and not just the public part of us. God doesn't see all the pretence that we have anyway, he understands what we are *really* like. It's important to be honest with him and to pray as if we really need him and not to pray as if we are doing him a favour. It seems that Smith took his challenges head on and would very rarely back off. But he wasn't alone. He spent so much time with God but he of course had other people around him. Yet it wasn't all plain sailing for Smith – he had some very tough times. Towards the end of his life, he suffered very badly from kidney stones and it has been reported that often he would be in intense pain and his underwear would be stained with blood as he was passing these stones, yet he would get up, preach and see people healed, and receive the Holy Spirit powerfully. Somehow in this suffering he managed to still be amazingly effective for God. Some of us don't really suffer a lot (I actually complained today about how rubbish our toaster was!) and some of us have enormous things in our lives to deal with. Somehow Smith was able to be used by God to see hundreds of people healed when he himself was not healed from poor eyesight and painful kidney stones. He was definitely tackling things head on.

> The real hero is always a hero by mistake; he dreams of being an honest coward like everybody else.
>
> (Umberto Eco, *Travels in Hyperreality*,
> Harcourt Brace, 1986)

Mr incredible crime-buster ...

We shouldn't go looking for stuff. We shouldn't go round looking for autopilot experiences, for ways that we can be have-a-go-heroes. Life will come to us anyway if we don't live in a bubble. If we live our lives in the usual places and with usual people, we will find that opportunities come about anyway. If we spend the whole time just sitting in front of the television, we probably won't experience very much, certainly first-hand anyway!

Even sometimes when a situation requires reaction, you have to make some sensible decisions. For example, I was shopping in Morrisons in Leeds with my kids, Rhea and Lauren. We parked the car and were getting a trolley when we heard somebody shout really loud and a car screech. A guy in a van had pulled out from the cash point, driving his car dangerously, pulled up outside the shop and then shouted and screamed at what appeared to be his wife near the door of the supermarket. Everyone stood still in amazement as he shouted, screamed and physically grabbed hold of her as she tried to walk away. I was a bloke with a sense of justice in me, and at that point wanted to say something to him or even give him the right hand of fellowship but I had my kids there, and no one to look after them, so it would have been irresponsible of me at that time to just make what would have been a selfish decision. I didn't feel good about not helping that day but there are times when we have to decide not to react ... but there are also times when we have to make tough choices.

I was at basketball practice one Friday having the usual mixed game when, to be honest, it got a bit 'arsey'. There was a lot of attitude flying around that night from everyone as the adrenalin was pumping around our bodies, and I had been playing for an hour or so, end to end, full-on basketball. This guy on the other team went up for a lay-up and he could jump miles higher than me. I couldn't block him, so I put my hand up to try and grab the ball as it went past me. As he flew past me, my hand hit him in the face and he missed the lay-up. I put my hand up to acknowledge that I had fouled him but something just snapped inside of him. He shouted, turned around and squared up to me. He started swearing, letting me know what would happen to me very soon. I was speechless at that point and just stood looking at him trying to diffuse the situation. Just as I thought he was going to back down, boom, the next thing I knew I was on the floor with blood coming out of my mouth. He had gotten really close to me and head-butted me. A few of the guys ran around just to make sure he wasn't going to do anything else to me and a couple of guys tried to calm the situation down and then loads of them just walked off, some of them never to come back to basketball practice again.

Even after the fight, he was obviously really angry, walking around as people continued to play. He was in the corner of the room bouncing a ball really hard and just trying to deal with what he had done, I guess. This was my team and I wasn't going to leave it so I didn't walk off, and somehow with God's grace I didn't retaliate in any way (he was harder than me anyway!). But as I sat there on the bench with my T-shirt, which had been torn off as he grabbed hold of me, and a towel to my mouth stopping the blood from my cut lip and nose from the head-butt, I realised that I had a decision to make. I realised that this could have escalated and as it was an ethnically diverse club could quite easily turn into a racial issue. So as he was stomping around the court bouncing a ball on his own, I decided to walk up and talk to him. Nervously, and a bit in shock, I went up to him and said, 'Look mate, you know that I'm a Christian and I just need you to know that I forgive you for what you just did to me.' He acknowledged what I said but didn't really say too much and I just left it like that. I got a shower, then went home, trying to decide if I would ever play again.

A few days later I was at a gig in Leeds, seeing Jazzy Jeff DJing. I was on my own, watching one of my hero DJs. I went to the bar for a drink and there was a tap on my shoulder. I turned round to see that it was this lad from basketball who had hit me. There were a few seconds silence, that seemed like an hour, while he checked me out, and I noticed that he had his mates behind him looking at me! I was really nervous and definitely needed the toilet at that point (!), but he said, 'Look mate, I'm really sorry for what I did. I'm sorry that I ripped your T-shirt, I'm sorry I was out of order. I had had a bad week', etc., and then he gave me a manly hug and offered to buy me a drink which I gratefully accepted. I still see this guy around and it's OK now, there is no hassle between us and we can get on, no problems. But I realise as I look back that I wasn't on autopilot after the head-butt, I just knew that I had to make a choice about how I reacted to the situation. So thankfully I decided that I had to forgive him there and then. I had to make a conscious decision to forgive him there and then, and try to defuse the situation, otherwise it would have turned into something worse. I can honestly say there were no 'holy feelings', there were no feelings of being close to God at that point, I just knew that it was practical and sensible for me to make the right choice and decide to reach out to him, and show him some of God's forgiveness.

(Please understand that I am not for a second comparing myself to Smith Wigglesworth by any stretch of the imagination, but a real story like that just brings our faith into reality.)

Craig Gross says, 'You can't blame the dark for being dark, you have to blame the light for not shining on it.'

Smith Wigglesworth gave this challenge to Christians:

> Live ready. If you have to get ready when the opportunity comes your way, it will be too late. Opportunity does not wait, not even while you pray. You must not have to get ready, you must live ready at all times.
>
> Be filled with the Spirit; that is, be soaked with the Spirit. Be so soaked that every thread in the fabric of your life will have received the requisite rule of

the Spirit then when you are misused and squeezed to the wall all that will ooze out of you will be the nature of Christ.

Help us God.

For the keenies and the groups ...

- Can you think of a situation that has required you to make a conscious decision to do the right thing?
- Would God 'ooze out of you' if you were pressed hard?
- Would you like to be more like Smith Wigglesworth? Why or why not? (See www.lfis.org/hero for more notes on Smith.)
- Do you think autopilot is the real us?
- How can we learn to 'live ready'?

Wheresoever you go, go with all your heart.

(Confucius (551–479 BC))

Women need a reason to have sex. Men just need a place.

(Billy Crystal)

This chapter was written by my Dad, Peter Jackson about a year before he died from an Asbestos related cancer (Mesothelioma) which he didn't know he had at the time of writing - which was just after he had retired. He died just after the book was published and one of his last journeys away from home was to the launch of our book in Leeds, a memory I will always treasure. I have left my Dad's chapter in the book as a tribute to him, his down-to-earth-faith and great sense of humour. I count it a privilege to have a Dad that I am proud of.

Lee Jackson September 2008

23

Old-Age Pensioner!

PETER JACKSON

Let me ask you two questions ...

1) Can you remember what they used to call the BBC radio stations before they had numbers?
2) Can you remember all the words to any Beatles song?

If you can answer these questions then you are probably retired or heading towards retirement. In 2004, I was in the same situation.

On Sunday evening, I was the vicar of the parish and a leader of a thriving church in the inner city. I was chair of school governors and chair of the board of trustees for the various projects that the church was supporting as a limited company and a registered charity. I was representative on various committees both in the church and in the city. I was communicating with local government regarding inner city regeneration and pastoring the many problems that are a normal part of everyday life with the people of God. I was leading a church that was attempting to reach out to those people who did not know Jesus or who did not want to know Jesus.

On the Monday morning, I was an old-age pensioner.

On the Sunday evening, Avril and I attended the farewell do that the church kindly put on for us. Many friends from many years and places in the past were there. It was a tearful, joyful evening of speeches and commendations.

On the Sunday, I was carrying the keys to the church and to the office doors. I was an ordained minister and priest in the Church of England, the licensed vicar to a parish of 8,000 people. I was an employer of various people in the Youth Project and the UK Online computer project.

On the Monday morning, I was carrying my bus pass.

Life in retirement had begun

Is that the end, then? Is it all finished? The question for a man of my generation is, 'Are you what you do and achieve or are you who you are?' We all know the answer in our heads but what about in our lives and in our hearts? What about when paid employment ceases? Is God's power at work in retirement? Avril and I had attended retirement preparation courses. But they were mainly about housing and finance with little spiritual input. The question remained.

God had always been at work in my life up to then. I came to Jesus about 30 years ago through a man called David Watson. I was baptised in the Holy Spirit at the end of the 1970s. Avril and myself have seen God do some amazing things. I have lived through a lot of church history. I have been around when choruses were first sung in church, fought the battle to get dance and drama in worship, made the case for modern Bible translations, dared to ask the Holy Spirit into his congregation. Avril and I lived through changes that are now part of normal church life. But the question is, is that it? Does God retire when we do? Is God's power at work in retirement or does he stop working in our lives when we stop full-time work?

A good friend had asked me to preach on this subject in his church so I had to consider the question. There is nothing like a deadline to concentrate the mind.

Is God's power at work in retirement?

I looked in Scripture – but nobody really retires there. You never hear of Jesus going to a retirement do and turning the water into wine. Most people in Scripture are either martyred, which I hope God was not calling me to, or just vanish from the scene, which I do not want to do either. I still think I have something to contribute.

I considered Moses. He spent 40 years as a somebody in Egypt. Then 40 years as a nobody in the desert and another 40 years to show how God could make a somebody out of a nobody – but he didn't retire. On Mount Nebo in Jordan, Moses hands over the power of leadership to the younger Joshua. But he does not retire, he dies and nobody knows where they buried him. We were on Mount Nebo in the year 2000 with Don MacLean and the BBC *Good Morning Sunday* team. Avril and I were helping to lead the pilgrimage and were guiding a coach full of pilgrims through the Holy Land in Israel/Palestine and Jordan. We stood on Mount Nebo and I said to my group, 'Moses stood here and looked across to the Promised Land.' They all turned and we looked across to the place where Jesus died and lived but you could not see a thing! The mist had come down and the Promised Land was not in sight. A local guide followed our gaze and said to me, 'It's always like this.'

This is how I felt on retirement. Many people long for retirement and see it as their promised land. As a happy workaholic, I had different feelings. I could not see where

I was going. The promised land was not in view. There was a mist that covered the future and I could not see through it.

Avril and I decided we would spend six months just looking round the local churches to try to find a spiritual home. We were looking for a church where the gospel was preached, the welcome warm and where we were allowed to laugh as well as cry. Some churches were welcoming, the people were lovely but we felt we would not be fed there or challenged. In some churches, the gospel was being preached but there did not seem to be the freedom of spirit that is part of the good news. Some churches were just too far away. Some were just unwelcoming.

I was reminded of a verse from Jer. 29:11: '"For I know the plans I have for you," declares the Lord, "plans to prosper you and not to harm you, plans to give you hope and a future."' I knew that hope and that future were for all time until you meet him in heaven. I knew in my head that God's promises do not end at a certain time, like when you have children or when you get a busy job or when you retire. But those promises had not filtered down to my heart. The way ahead was still misty.

To my shame and Avril's embarrassment, I also realised that I was not a very good 'old person'. I objected noisily when someone tried to patronise me or treat me like an idiot. We went to the movies, to a Wednesday afternoon matinee at a special price for 'senior citizens'. Before the movie started, the manager came to the front to speak to us in a loud voice, speaking slowly and precisely. The movie was *Gangs of New York*, a brilliant Martin Scorsese film. The manager apologised that the movie may be too noisy for us and a bit bloodthirsty. 'I know you don't like that sort of thing.' And, as it was a long movie, he said that there would be a toilet break in the middle. I was rising to my feet to say something really cutting and incredibly witty when Avril told me to sit down, please! I know he meant well but remember the scripture that Lee pointed us to in Proverbs? That grey hair is the beauty of age not necessarily the sign of the mentally deficient. I know at the time this was part of my not liking to be considered an OAP, but perhaps more of the over 65s should follow suit ...

Time went by and I was at last beginning to settle into retirement. I found it a great blessing to be relieved of reading, organising or writing agendas, minutes and rotas. I realised the pleasure that seeing more of my wife, my grown-up children and grandchildren brought. But spiritually, I just needed another sign from God after the Jeremiah piece – just to clear that mist a little bit. I found it in my daily Scripture readings, or rather it found me:

> O God, you have taught me from my earliest childhood, and I have constantly told others about the wonderful things you do. Now that I am old and grey, do not abandon me, O God. Let me proclaim your power to this new generation, your mighty miracles to all who come after me.
>
> (Ps. 71:17,18, NLT)

As long as there is a new generation, then God needs you as well as all those youth workers, even if you have grey hair and creaky knees. In the Old Testament, the young and the old sat together round the campfires and shared the stories from their past. We have no campfires now and the young and the old rarely sit together. In a century where new is always better and where the old are not respected, we rarely even sit around the TV. We form age-based ghettos and attempt to keep each other out. It is safer that way and none of us have to think about community or death. But we who have a little more time can seek opportunities to tell how God has worked in our lives and how he will work in the future. We can tell anyone who will listen that we do not know all the answers but at least we are asking the same questions.

You may not be as active as you once were but you are needed today more than ever. In a world that turns its back on God, he still needs us, all of us, to chat and gossip about him. And if they call us old bores, will you be a bore for Christ? Paul was pleased to be a fool.

> He will turn the hearts of the fathers to their children,
> and the hearts of the children to their fathers; or else
> I will come and strike the land with a curse.
>
> (Mal. 4:6, NIV)

I have learned that there is one word that fills the retired person with joy. One word that we are always looking for: that word is 'concessions'. It means that we can take the grandchildren on the crazy golf and not pay full price. It means if we can get in the café before a certain time, then the coffee is cheaper. I came to realise that there are no concessions in God's kingdom or God's service. There are no allowances made for age or for anything else. We were all commissioned in Mt. 28 to do what we can when we can. Jesus didn't say, 'I will be with you always *to the day you retire.*' He said, 'I will be with you always *to the end of the age.*'

It is a new season, a new time, an exciting time. We have at last found a warm church where a gracious minister welcomed us and where we hear the good news and are challenged and loved – and used. I can preach the gospel when I am asked without bothering about the heating or the council meeting. This is what God called me to do all those years ago and now I can do it.

If your hair is grey and you are one of the twerlies,[1] let me encourage you. I know you may tire of all the talk in the church about the young and the future. They may have the future but we have something equally precious: we have a past, we have experience and, most importantly, we have time. We have time to share how God has worked with us and to encourage anybody younger to take a chance and see how God will work with them.

And if you are part of this generation, someone will come along in 40 years' time and ask you, 'What group was the youngest to get a No. 1 album in 2005?' (McFly!); 'Can you remember the Crazy Frog?'; 'Can you still remember how to text using your fingers on one of those "old fashioned" mobile phones?'

'If you can answer this,' he'll say, 'you must be retired or nearing retirement and I'm talking to you.'

Note

[1] A twerlie is an OAP with a bus pass. The bus pass is only valid for reduced fairs after 9.30 a.m. If you come before that you are too early: you are a twerlie.

If you want to make God laugh tell him your future plans.

(Woody Allen)

24

Baz I Am

BAZ GASCOYNE

May of 1975 was unbelievable. The government appointed a 'Drought Secretary'. I had to share a bath with my brother and we were encouraged to only flush the loo once a day. It was the beginning of a 16-month dry spell in the UK, the longest ever recorded for England and Wales since 1727. But it was for another reason it was to become a year forever etched in my memory.

It started out just like any other school day. Up at 5.30 a.m. to do my milk round, home, washed, breakfast and catching the 8.10 a.m. Number 6 bus to school with my mates.

On my return home, I could never have imagined what I was going to hear when I arrived at my grandparents'. I knew something was up as soon as I arrived, as my mam was sat in the room with my gran. I never had a welcoming committee unless I was in trouble. 'Now what have I done?' I thought or 'Who's died?' My mam began by saying that they had something to tell me. I could see she was nervous and looking quite agitated which seemed to intensify the nervous pounding of my heart. What was I going to hear? Nothing or no one could have prepared me for what I was about to hear. 'You are going to Africa for three months, son.'

'What do you mean Africa? Why?'

'To see your dad.'

'You're kidding right? Why would I want to go and see him?' I replied. 'You can sod off.'

It was very rare that I would reply like this to Mam with out receiving a swift crack around the back of my head. My gran tried to calm me down but I couldn't understand why they would want me to go.

Why did I react like this? Because in my 15 years, I had only seen him a handful of times since he had gone to live and work in Zambia in the early sixties. I could see from my mam's eyes that she was not happy but my gran stepped in. 'You'll have to go as the tickets are bought and your cousin Alex is going with you to look after you.'

Great, not only was I being forced to go and see a man I'd hardly seen, I had to go with my southern posh git of a cousin. Could the day get any better?

My gran was upset. 'It will give you chance to get to know your dad.' I didn't want to get to know him. Anyway, he had not made much of an effort to get to know me over the last 15 years. It was very difficult for me to get excited about the pending trip. How was I going to develop a relationship with someone I didn't really know? This must have been hard for my gran as my dad was her son, but I couldn't pretend to be excited about this even for her sake.

Well, July was here and I was in Northampton at my cousin Alex's parents' house on the eve of the journey to South Africa. As I laid my head on the pillow, I hoped that this awful nightmare would end. But next morning we were driven to Southampton where we boarded the *Sa Vaal* ship and entered our three berth cabin that I would share with Alex for the next 17 days as we sailed to Africa. Alex and I could not have been more different if we tried. He was one of three children from a wealthy family. His dad was a very successful businessman who didn't talk with a plum in his mouth but what seemed more like a cricket ball. I could never understand a word he said but when he laughed after a sentence I knew this was my cue to do the same. He was a nice guy. I was from a humble working class family, with my mam working all hours to support my brother and me. She has always been a good worker.

Alex was 19 years old and was attending Reading University, 'The third best university in the country' as he recently reminded me tongue in cheek. He used to call me a 'thick northern lad' who would not achieve anything. Fair enough, considering I used to call him a 'pompous southern posh git'.

So with me thinking what I did of him, and him me, we slowly left Southampton harbour.

Looking back now, I did quite enjoy the cruise and have some amusing memories. That first night, Alex took me around all the bars on the ship. For every drink he had, I would have a half pint of beer and by the end of the evening I was very drunk. I can still recall waking up the next morning totally naked, flashing my manhood in a bed of sick and urine, and the porter for our room informing me later he had put a plastic sheet on my mattress for my problem!

Alex once got arrested for going up to the first class quarters. And on one evening, we ate our way through the whole dinner menu a second time as Alex felt the waiter was rushing us to finish early.

As we arrived in Durban, we knew we were being met by a lady called Christine who wore brown spectacles, my dad's girlfriend. I did think this was going to be a huge challenge finding her with all the people disembarking the ship as well as all the people at the harbour side waiting to greet the passengers. However, Alex and I were delayed getting off the ship for about one to two hours as there was something wrong with our passports. Looking back, I wouldn't be surprised if it was the crew's way of getting back at us for the things Alex and I got up to during the cruise. Even though they might have thought it was going to cause some hassle, it actually helped us. As we left the ship, there was only one lady with brown spectacles and a face that looked like thunder having been kept waiting so long.

After spending some time in Durban, Johannesburg and Malawi, we were on our way to Ndola, Zambia. Apprehension began to consume me as I played over and over again in my mind the inevitable meeting of father and son. Unfortunately, one more thing was going to add to the tension that was building inside me. We had been flying approximately 20 minutes when the pilot pulled aside the curtain that separated him from the passengers and very casually asked, 'Where is the engineer?' over and over again. One of the propellers was stopping and starting like an old gramophone winding down and then being quickly wound up again. The only music playing here was a young lady across the aisle holding a baby, screaming, 'We're going to die!' It was like some dreadful out-take from *Airplane*.

The plane landed and my underpants needed changing. Eventually, we were off the plane and walking in the dark towards a shed which I was surprisingly excited about. That was soon to change as this man I hardly knew came up saying, 'Hello, son,' as he hugged me. I felt so cold, embarrassed and empty inside as I said, 'Alright' in a nonchalant 15-year-old way, equivalent to today's, 'Whatever'. We all got into the vehicle and headed out of the small airport towards the farm where we would be staying on Mufilira Road.

How long would I have to stay here and how long before I was back to normality, back in Darlington in the UK? As we drove along the dirt track, I wondered what this time in Ndola was going to reveal. Where did he live? What did he do? What happened to his previous wife? Would we get on? Why did he leave my mam and me? What were Alex and I going to do? So many questions.

My experience there was to leave a lasting impression on me and I would carry negative feelings about Zambia around with me for the next 30 years. I can still remember the house, the bedroom Alex and I shared. The many bottles of cold tonic water I drank due to the heat. The swimming pool that I enjoyed each day and where I pretended to try and drown young Stephen making him cry and swallow a large amount of chlorine. Why? Because I did not like him calling my dad 'Dad', even though he had not been a dad to me.

I was shocked by the way the black people were treated and I would sneak steaks and good food to them when we were having barbeques, or brays as the Zambians called them.

One day my dad produced this thick rope which he told us was a noose with which he used to hang people. He was employed by the Zambian government to hang criminals. Someone had to do this job but why him and why not someone else? Why did it seem like he enjoyed it?

The longer I was there the more I wanted to get out of the place as quickly as possible and this drove me to pray to God earnestly for the first time in my life. I was not a follower of Jesus at the time, but I thought I needed some help as I did not feel safe in the home and I wanted to get back to the UK. I remember kneeling on the lounge floor and saying something like the following to God: 'God, I'm not sure even if you exist but I remember singing about you and to you at junior school and learning how you rescued people who were in danger. If you are around please can you get me out of this mess? I want to go back home.'

A few nights later a few of my dad's friends came around and one of them asked, 'So when do you go back to the UK?'

'As soon as possible,' I replied which was followed by Alex spurting out his drink all over the floor and my dad saying something like, 'Well, if that's how you feel you might as well go.'

To which I replied, 'Good.' And within a week Alex and I were back on a plane heading for London.

Wow, had God heard my prayer or was this just a coincidence? Whichever, I was very grateful.

When the plane landed at Heathrow I wondered if I would ever go back to that country. One thing was for sure, it would not be to go and see my dad.

As I write this chapter I am 46 days away from placing my feet on Zambian soil once again where I will be asking God to bless and heal the land.

It was in 1994 that I first started having thoughts that I should return to Zambia but it took many years before I was in a position to go back and make my peace with a country that held so much turmoil for me.

In 1995, St Thomas Crooke's Church in Sheffield hosted a conference entitled 'Discovering the Father's Heart'. Regardless of rights and wrongs, anyone whose father has been absent could tell you of the hole it leaves and the yearning to be fathered. I went to the front of the church and knelt down, desperate to discover the Father's heart for myself and allow God to deal with my feelings towards my earthly father. As I knelt there, I had a mental picture of a gravestone with the letters R.I.P. and my father's head above it. Whilst I still had my eyes closed, Mike Bickle, one of the speakers at the conference, placed his hand on my head and said, 'This man will never have a hold on your life again.' At that point, the picture in my mind exploded, like some sci-fi film when an asteroid collides with another, and disappeared. How did Bickle know what was going on? The love of God, eager to speak to me, and let me know that the past didn't have to influence my ability to receive my Heavenly Father's love. An overwhelming love, peace and excitement came over me, which was tested the next time I visited my mam and she gave her usual throwaway comment, 'You're just like your dad, you.' I waited for the words to penetrate my heart, for my usual defensiveness to rise, but nothing. God had set me free.

And so the thoughts continued about revisiting Zambia. I heard stories of others going to places and praying for the land, standing in the gap for events that had taken place in the past, and am grateful to Roger Mitchell's wise counsel: 'Don't try and make this happen. If this is God, he will lead and show when and how this is to be.'

The new millennium arrived, and one Sunday morning our friend Godfrey Birtill was leading a morning of worship with us. We were praying for our nation and I was lying on a Union Jack flag when Godfrey began singing over me about Zambia and going back there in the future. The children started to wrap me up in the flag and I began to feel a huge amount of pain and sorrow. A lady in the church, who loves doing anagrams, immediately saw potential in the word Zambia: 'Baz, I am'.

Was this coincidence or God encouraging me that he was calling and reminding me that he is faithful.

And so over the next couple of years, I began to look for opportunities to visit, ever mindful of Roger Mitchell's advice, and trusting that the right time would present itself clearly, until in 2004 our friends Pete and Samie came to stay and we discovered Samie's parents were living in Ndola, the very town in Zambia I had visited as a child.

God was really prodding, pulling, pushing now, and I took the email contact to get in touch with her parents.

And so the decision was made. In 2005 we were going with a team to Tanzania to visit Ian and Andie Wilson ('Missionary? Me?') and it seemed the perfect opportunity to fly on afterwards and stay with Samie's parents in Zambia. What would the trip look like? We had no idea, but we knew this was something we needed to do.

Once we'd made our decision, the confirmations (or ~~co~~God-incidences) came in thick and fast. Linda and I spent a whole day preparing our cellar prayer rooms for another church 24/7 prayer week. The white material draped down the walls and the ceilings were covered and we stood back to admire our handiwork. Something ruined the pure white effect, and I bent down to remove the offending item: a small stamp from Zambia with the picture of an eagle and the year 1975. Of course, this was my stamp from the year of my first visit. But how had it got there, and why that stamp, out of all the stamps that could have fallen out of my old stamp album?

One Sunday in May, Linda and I went to join the J2 event – a gathering of 1,000 young people to pray for our nation, which our friends John and Maria O'Brian pioneered. We arrived during the break so chatted with a few people. I saw a friend called Graham and asked him how he was. 'Good but tired' was his reply and I discovered he had just returned from a trip to Ndola, Zambia. He told me a story about a blue butterfly which held key memories for him in relation to Zambia, and then gave me a blue plastic butterfly which someone had previously given to him.

The following month, there were two half-page articles with large photos in our national press entitled 'Return of the Blue Butterfly' and 'Return of the Blues'. The articles reported that the blue butterfly, not seen in the UK since the seventies, had returned. 'Beautiful butterfly that came back from the dead', 'resurrection of the blue butterfly' and 'the stunning Large Blue is flying high again'. Once again, God had grabbed my attention.

That same month, I was at a city youth event in Sheffield called 'Nail the Truth'. I was tired and emotionally exhausted from the week's activities, so decided to walk round the hall praying for the evening. While I was walking around, a young man called David approached me and said he felt God had given him a word for me. He had seen me with an eagle's face and then said what he thought it meant. An eagle, the picture on the Zambian stamp found in our prayer cellar, and the symbol on the Zambian national flag!

I began to feel like one of the McFly family from *Back to the Future*. It was as if God was saying, 'Hello, McFly, is there anyone there?' as the godly coincidences and small signs stacked up.

On 23 June, whilst praying and reading my Bible, I felt God might be asking me to fast for 40 days before the trip and that the number 40 was significant to this trip.

Now of course the number 40 in the Bible is very significant. It rained 40 days and nights in Noah's day. Isaac was 40 when he married Rebecca. Moses was with God on the mount for 40 days and nights. Goliath presented himself to Israel for 40 days. God gave Nineveh 40 days to repent. Jesus fasted for 40 days, he was tempted for 40 days and he remained on the earth 40 days after resurrection, to name but a few. So I decided to fast TV and alcohol for the 40 days leading up to our trip.

And so into July, and we're preparing for our trip, with Linda in her usual way reading travel guides. She reads to me from the *Bradt Travel Guide to Zambia*: 'Zambia lies landlocked between the tropic of Capricorn and the equator, shaped like a *giant butterfly* and covering about 752,610 km.' Hello, is anyone there?

The day of the fast begins and I'm hoovering our bedroom carpet when I notice a stamp on the floor. You're probably ahead of me by now. This one was of a picture of an aeroplane taking off with the words 'Zambian Airways'. 'God, how are these stamps falling out of my stamp album into strategic places?' I had no idea, but knew that God was pressing home a point about this trip.

I begin writing this chapter and discover from my old school report that I missed 40 days of school for the visit to Africa.

I come across my old passport. Looking at the hard-faced young boy, I discovered that the date I left Zambia was 17 September 1975, the date of our first full day in Zambia 30 years on.

And soon it's September. As the plane begins to taxi down the runway to leave Mwanza in Tanzania and head for Dar es Salaam, images of the previous 14 days come to mind. The wonderful time on safari in the Serengeti; the hugely generous and faithful people of KVCC church; the great team from Derby and my friends from the Eccles giving themselves 150 per cent to everything that was asked of them, and my friend Gary who led the team superbly and survived working with me!

The challenges and excitement of seeing over 300 people become Christians as they heard about Jesus on the streets; the struggles with the culture, wondering if they would all end up disciples and whether they were genuine in their response to Jesus; the first 50 baptised on our last Sunday; the freedom in worship and the manliness of the men dancing; the celebrations when people became Christians.

Sunday evenings visiting the 'Maskini' (poor people) with Dr Samuel and his team who have faithfully visited these people for ten years sharing the love of Jesus and providing food. Shaking hands with people whose hands are leprous stumps and stuttering over the Swahili phrases for 'hello' and 'God bless you'; watching with pride as Heather and Emily from our team speak of Jesus' love to the watching group and seeing first hand the great work Ian and Andie Wilson of Bridge2aid are doing.

And so onto Dar for the first stage of our journey to Zambia, which ends in a 36-seater plane late Friday afternoon 16 September.

> Well, Father,
> Thanks for getting us this far and all we have
> experienced already.
> Once we get to Zambia, will you please lead us to
> the places we need to visit,
> The people we need to meet,
> The prayers we need to walk and say,
> The places we need to avoid,
> The people we need to avoid.
> Help us to do and say all that we need to do in the
> next five days.
> So please lead and direct us by your Spirit.
> Amen.

On the last stage of our journey, I have a niggling thought that God is asking me to do something when we land at Ndola. I turn to Linda for encouragement who laughs when I tell her I think God is asking me to kiss the ground when I arrive. 'Yes, I was thinking the very same thing a couple of days ago.' Hello, is there anyone there?

We eventually land and wait until everyone else is off the plane. Thanking the crew, I walk down the stairs feeling apprehension and excitement rushing through every vein of my body. At the foot of the stairs, I turn to the staff: 'Hope you don't mind but I need to do something as it is 30 years since I was last in your country.' I knelt down, aware of people watching me from the bus full of passengers and airport staff, and kissed the land, believing I was going to see God kiss this land in many different ways over the next few days.

And so, Saturday morning 17 September 2005, 30 years on to the day from my departure from Zambia as a young boy, Tony who we are staying with, is driving us the two and a half hour journey south to Kabwe to a prayer summit that Emmanuel Kure had invited us to.

Eventually, we arrive and find the venue where we are treated like royalty by these lovely people who had never met us before and didn't know why we were there. Tony arranged to pick us up at 12.30 and we were taken to meet Papa Billy, a large and colourful chap in his lime-green suit who was the leader of the church hosting the summit. They sat us at the front of the meeting, the only white people among a gathering of approximately 500 black Zambians.

The banner above the stage read 'Kabwe Prayer summit 2005: Ultimate Recovery and Occupation. Speaker Dr Emmanuel Kure from Nigeria.'

The worship band were playing and Papa Billy began singing 'Heal Our Land' and the crowd began singing this over and over again. I was beginning to feel like God had set us up when Kure came in and welcomed us both with his lovely smile and hug.

Many of the Zambians were wearing skirts or shirts of the Zambian flag with the words 'Celebrating 40 years of independence' and the words 'Freedom, peace and pride'. There it was again, the number 40.

The worship was amazing and the presence of God tangible. I looked at Linda and like me she was crying:

for some reason God was allowing us to be at a significant event for Zambia. Eventually the worship ended and Emmanuel Kure was invited to prophesy over the nation of Zambia on the last day of this summit.

He commented that people will have noticed that they had some visitors among them, and then told how we had met in Sheffield in 2004 when he led a prayer summit in our city. He informed the people that we were on a journey with God and invited us onto the stage and to tell the people why we were in Zambia. I thought, 'Great, what do we do now, God?' I smiled, always a good thing to do when you are stood in front of a hall of people you do not know.

I told them about my visit to Zambia 30 years previously and that it didn't hold happy memories for me. I told them how I'd felt about what I had seen at that time, of how the way some of the white people treated the black people wasn't right or acceptable. I told them how I'd felt uncomfortable with my dad's occupation as hangman. I told how I felt God had led me to return to make peace with the land. So Linda and I knelt, grabbed some soil and prayed that God would bless and heal this land from past atrocities of the white man, reversing and redeeming what had been stolen. When I handed the microphone back to Emmanuel he asked all the people in the hall who knew they or their family members had been negatively impacted by the white man to step forward.

As Linda and I stood at the side of the stage, nothing could have prepared us for what we were about to witness and experience. Dozens of people came to the front, sadness etched on their faces and mirrored in their eyes. This was a holy moment and I was pleased to be part of it. I prayed on behalf of the white people; a member of the congregation prayed on behalf of the black people. Prayers of repentance, forgiveness and healing. I don't think I have ever prayed a more serious prayer in my whole life.

I now understood a bit more what the people of Nabutauta in Fiji were doing in 2004 when they asked for forgiveness for the actions of their people when they killed and ate an English missionary in 1867. They publicly apologised to family members of the missionary in the presence of the Fijian Prime Minister as they believed their land had been cursed ever since and it needed healing. You can read more about this on: http://news.bbc.co.uk/1/hi/world/asia-pacific/3263163.stm

An old man came up to me and thanked me, saying today he had been healed and set free from the pain. As I stood there and hugged him, I knew that this was God's timing. Then I remembered 'Baz I am'.

I wanted to go back to the house where my dad had lived and I had visited 30 years previously, so Tony did some detective work and we were given details of the address. To my amazement, the sign at the front of the farm read 'Zambian Boys' Brigade Headquarters'. As we drove up the driveway, the house looked smaller than I remembered but everything was where I remembered it being. Tony explained briefly to the family now living in the house why I was there and they were happy for me to explore and spend some time in the garden. So we walked round, sat in the pool (now filled in) and prayed: 'Let the object of the Boys' Brigade be true in that place – the advancement of Christ's kingdom among boys and the promotion of habits, obedience and reverence and all that tends towards true Christian manliness.' As we sat and poured oil into the ground, we expected there to be a process of spiritual redemption and healing, to reflect the farm's physical change of purpose, and an ending of the negative memories and ties I had held since my trip in the seventies. For the first time, I was able to genuinely pray and release my dad into God's blessing, understanding that God's love for each of us is the same. As we drove away, I knew that after 30 years there had been closure.

Linda and I are two ordinary people, following our convictions. Yet we are also two people following the finger of God. As a friend of ours says, when you take ordinary people and add in the Holy Spirit, the result can be explosive. Subsequently, our prayer is that we see and hear about changes over the next few years, not just in our own lives but in the nation of Zambia. Not because we are anyone special but because God is huge, and his healing has consequences that go far beyond anything we can imagine.

Questions

- Are there events or memories from your past about which God is saying, 'Now is the time to bring closure'? Will you allow him to do this?
- Is God calling, 'Hello, is anyone there?' Don't ignore him.
- Is there anywhere you need to revisit from your past?

Want to be an effective church? Have more parties.

25

Living with Autism

NICK JEFFERY

I guess it was inevitable. I've always been aware of my eccentric tendencies! I'm drawn to familiar things and places, you know, holiday locations, particular chairs, food types, needing things to be in reasonable routine and order. Let's just say ... well no, let my wife confirm, I've always had autistic tendencies! So when, in March 1996, our third child Oliver appeared in the world, I should not have been at all surprised that he was autistic.

This is the first time that I have *ever* sat down and begun to record my experiences and emotions about living with Oliver. We've talked about it as a family, my wife Jane and our daughters, Laura and Alice, aged 21 and 17 respectively, were OK about this stab at a bit of reflective writing, so here we go! This, by the way, is not a story of a 'Von Trapp' style superhuman Christian family seeing amazing miracles and saintly responses at every corner. Sorry, I'm writing this from my perspective, a male one, just to say that it is possible to survive in extreme situations!

Now, let me work on some definitions for you here, in case you're reading this thinking, 'Oh bless, maybe Oli is lacking eye contact, rather withdrawn but almost certainly, fantastic at art and a concert-standard pianist.'

Well, we all watch too many telly programmes about that sort of high functioning, 'Asperger's' level autism. My son, Oliver, is extremely autistic. On the spectrum, he's at the far far end, the end that includes severe learning difficulties, the end that includes limited language, self-harming and incontinence. The end of the spectrum that, generally, people never see because the truth is that families and carers of significantly autistic children do not go out, mix, socialise, have lots of friends, go on outings or get invited out to children's parties! They become 'hard to reach groups', families that withdraw with little support, and grow old together gracefully, well ungracefully, ageing prematurely, parents having significant mental and physical difficulties because of the sheer pressure of unsustainable lifestyles without support or respite.

OK, got that off my chest! So, that is the picture for many, but not us, really, not us! It is not our experience or lifestyle choice! We live with a beautiful, loving, amazing, friend of Jesus, severely autistic son, called Oliver. We have not withdrawn, we do go out 'everywhere' and we have some brilliant friends. But it has been very hard. The battle with God along the 'why us?' line, the occasional patronising Christian who thinks we are fantastic for adopting a disabled kid – hold me back someone! The church that told us that Oli was not being healed because of our lack of faith.

And my daily wrestle with God because deep down I want a relationship with a growing son that involves two-way conversation, a son I can take to see Portsmouth FC without him running onto the pitch during the game – oh yes, it really happened!

And the need for acceptance that he may not develop further than his current mental age of two years six months and he may be at home with us ... always! And the huge grapple with God over the healing thing, 'Please God, do it today, just in an instance, make him whole.' But then I look at this happy little boy worshipping in church and think, Lord, make me whole.

So, we make the best of it, have fantastic family times together, watch my brilliant girls and beautiful wife loving him and caring for him and chasing him and changing his nappies and apologising! You know, we spend most of our time apologising, all the time, everywhere, I introduce myself as, 'Hi, I'm Nick and I'm sorry' – although for those that know me, I need to apologise for my own behaviour not Oli's!!

It is possible to survive, to make it through, to retain your health, sanity and faith, but only just and it's not easy. There are no quick fix solutions to living with disability. You need to find a level of sustainable lifestyle, you've got to be confident in yourself and in God, and you have to be thick-skinned, because people say some really dumb things. But you must *not* withdraw. Stay in contact, be part of Christian community, make Christian brothers and sisters learn about autism, become pushy and demanding of your needs.

So we decided to engage fully with normal everyday life – there were just too many reasons why we should stay at home with Oliver, withdraw, keep him away from the risks and dangers of the outside world and other people … nah, no challenge there, so we got out there to see what would happen. We joined sports clubs, The National Trust, attended museums, art galleries, concerts, cinema trips, shopping, you name it, we've been there and even gone back!

The National Trust is great: old houses, priceless furniture, crystal and extremely elderly staff, what could possibly go wrong? Well, nothing actually. Now Oli loves art galleries, castles and old houses, he just won't wait patiently, so he's always pushing in, normally pushing people's bottoms and they always think it's me and it never is – honest!

So, what is the secret of surviving with autism?

1) A sense of humour – which I appreciate is dangerous in church sometimes!
2) The ability to talk together as a family about what is going on.
3) The ability to talk together with God about what is going on!
4) Having the ability to risk assess in a way that won't make you conclude it's safer to stay at home – because there is always risk if you leave the house with an autistic child.
5) Know your exit, the ability to cut your losses, operate at a damage limitation level and just get out while you're ahead!
6) As a dad, stay with it, engage with your family, talk about it and remember big tough guy, it really is OK to cry!

So that is the secret formula. It's not big, or clever, it's not rocket science, just commitment, love and common sense. If you have those ingredients, you're ready to deal with extreme situations.

Just a couple of random thoughts about support services and agencies; this is not a rant because I work in education with young people so I know how difficult it is to engage with families. But don't let anyone insist you make the disabled person take drugs! For two years, Oliver was on anti-depressants – he was five at the time. The school insisted and the consultant complied. They were not for his health just his behaviour. Jane and I believed God wanted us to take him off the drugs. We no longer knew who our son really was – this was the drugged-up version. How could we pray for his healing or know who he really was? So we took him off the drugs and there were some side effects, but all of it was done with medical support, and after a few months we had the real drug-free Oliver. That was fine. Prone to tantrums and not sleeping, but fine! Not long afterwards, there was a lot of very bad press about this drug, so he would have been taken off it anyway! Thank you, God, for letting us do it early!

Dads, stay involved, be part of the family, don't withdraw or run. I know that it is really hard for dads to talk about how they really feel. There are few support services for dads, and the divorce rate among families of autistic children is much higher than the average. So dads, don't run, stay – your kids need you. You are a significant person and will be in the life of an autistic child. I had to learn that I had a role, not from my son or my family, but certainly from the Social Services. Even now, right now, despite what Jane and I tell them, I'm down in Oliver's Statement as an absent father! Hello! I'm here, at weekends, some evenings, at night! I work, but I am here. So dads, whatever the evangelical Christian term for, 'Don't let the buggers get you down' is, apply it! Stay and engage!

I talked about risk assessment and knowing your exit – vital, balanced formula that one! Recently we took Oli to Pizza Hut. We arrived, already knowing the restaurant layout, the risks, danger and culture.

Oli likes it there because if we sit by the window he can see boats going past on the river. He likes watching people and we can sit him in a corner. The meal went well, we relaxed, big mistake! My daughter took him to the disabled toilet, we stayed at the table talking. Out of the corner of my eye I became aware of Oliver moving towards us at very high speed, with his bag held out in front of him. He arrived at the table, put his bag on the surface and used it to push all the plates, glasses and cutlery, everything off the table! He was very excited by now, lots of noise, every eye on our table. As we picked up the mess Oli walked to the table next door. They had just received delivery of a giant deep pan farmhouse pizza. It was on a wooden base and the handle was over the edge of the table. I noticed the risk, Oli noticed the risk, sadly the happy family at the table did not notice the risk. So in slow motion fashion, I tried to dive around the table to reach their pizza, but Oli was ahead of me. I yelled, 'NO!', but it sounded like it was in slow motion, too. In one movement, Oli swiped the giant farmhouse deep pan pizza wooden base handle – it flew in the air in slow motion, flipping over and over as it flew up towards the ceiling. Every eye in the restaurant followed it as it landed splat, face down, on the floor! I have never seen so many waiting staff in one place at the same time as I did then – it was like a pizza delivery boy convention! As the staff fussed around, we applied principle number 2, you head for the exit! I paid, apologised to everyone, especially to the now traumatised giant farmhouse pizza-less family, and made the long walk through the restaurant towards the exit. Again it felt like slow motion, the walk felt half a mile and once again every eye was upon us. The restaurant was silent! So I stopped, looked back, smiled, waved and said, 'See you next week' in a most sincere voice!

Again, the principles not to forget are always risk assess and know your exit!

Like I said, we try to take Oliver everywhere. Last year, we attempted a rather ambitious trip to London to visit the Natural History Museum. It was doomed from the start. We should have aborted the mission, I should have read the signs of the times, I should have known better. We live in Norwich – 'C'mon, let's be having you', as someone once said – so we drove to Newbury Park to take the Underground. It was lovely, the empty train over ground, no problem. Then the train went underground, Oli started to get stressed. Then the train got very full and Oli had a crisis: screaming, kicking, all the usual things. As we pulled into a station, Oli grabbed for something to give him a bit more leverage to get away from me; it was the emergency cord! About 20 minutes later, the train moved on. I felt something in my spirit telling me that we were not that popular with our fellow commuters! A day at the museum, then back to the Underground. It was now 5 p.m. on a Saturday, a football Saturday, a very busy, no-room-on-the-train Saturday. So, in sterling fashion, we pushed our way to the front of the platform. I was carrying Oli as a guard pushed us into the world's most packed train, Oli screaming, distressed, the whole train watching as I held him in my arms. Then, he somehow slithered from my vice-like grip … he was on the floor, under people's feet, out of site … he was gone! I panicked, trying to find him in the carriage, crowds of people, swaying as the train sped towards the station. Thankfully, there was a happy ending. At the far end of the carriage, a huge Afro-Caribbean woman let out a blood-curdling scream. I looked across as, out of the blue, her skirt raised up. Oliver had crawled under her ample clothing and stood up so her skirt rose like a huge marquee tent! It was a scene of chaos! Anyway, we survived, though we've not been back on the Underground and I avoided eye contact with the woman!

The learning outcome: try most things once, but know when to quit or at least when to head for the exit!

So, finally, back to the church. I sometimes feel like we are co-existing with the church. It feels like they just don't know what to say. People will pat you on the back and say they don't know how you cope, but that's as far as it often goes. People are not sure how to help. I sympathise. Honestly, what can they do? But some, the few, will invite us for a meal; pray for us.

One person I will name. Chris Bowater, world famous worship leader! This year we took Oli to the Grapevine Christian Festival. We were in the big top, at the front, dancing to the worship. Oli ran away, he ran along the front row, past the B-list celebrities, you know, the ones that didn't make the platform. He stopped by the front screen; he was a bit in the way, standing in the wrong area, on the wrong side of the rope! Chris Bowater, international worship leader, saw Oliver, in the way, out of place. Chris came down from the stage, down the steps, stood by Oliver, and joined him in the dance! Oli loved it, later Chris hugged us both, told us he loved us with tears streaming down his face and returned to the A-list celebrities. Thank you, Chris, that is exactly what we need. People who are prepared to stand with us, you know, come to where we are, and love us. That is the Jesus Oli and I have grown to love. Whatever your circumstances, keep the humour and keep the faith!

Complete the following statement: 'Opera, ballet and line dancing are ...'

26

Peace in the Struggle

LEE JACKSON

The UK's favourite comedy programme is *Only Fools and Horses*. There are three famous clips from *Only Fools and Horses* that I often use when I am doing talks. There is Delboy in the bar, Batman and Robin and, the classic clip, Del and Rodney with the chandelier. The Trotter family pretended that they were experienced at renovating crystal chandeliers and get a job in a stately home. They try to remove the crystal chandeliers from the ceiling and send their grandad upstairs to remove the retaining bolts slowly as Delboy and Rodney stand on their ladders ready to catch the chandelier. The bolts slowly squeak as they brace themselves. Grandad hits a bolt to release the chandelier and only then do they realise that they are standing under the wrong chandelier and the next one further down the hallway smashes to the ground in a thousand pieces. A classic bit of British comedy.

I wonder why quite an average sitcom like *Only Fools and Horses* became so popular. Obviously, quality scripts and acting go a long way but there is also something endearing about the Trotters never quite making it (and even when they do they still mess it up) that really resonates with something in British culture. They seem to tick a box in all of us: Yeah, we are all plonkers and things don't often go quite as well as we had hoped them to; maybe we are not as clever as we want people to believe. We all embarrass ourselves more then we would like, bogies on our nose, breaking wind loudly in public, forgetting people's names, to name a few! Life doesn't always go to plan.

There are a few experiences that you have in life which change you for ever. One of mine happened while visiting Northern Ireland with YWAM. I had been working in Dundonald on a loyalist estate just before the ceasefire. I lived with a local family for a few weeks and loved the place, it was wonderful. The people and the food were fantastic! Work-wise, I was put in charge of the schools work module. We had a whole series of lessons to do in a school. We'd had an excellent week being involved in school life and we met some great people there. Sari, my friend from YWAM, and I had just finished giving a lesson and we left at the end of school with all the rest of the kids. We crossed the footbridge over the dual carriageway and started to make our way to our host's home, when suddenly I heard a noise behind me and saw what I thought was a bag flying up above the bonnet of a car. Something happened inside of me, and I realised that this wasn't a bag, it was a person. I somehow got across the dual carriageway to the other side of the road and made my way to the scene of the accident, without thinking twice. A young man of 18 was lying there in the road with blood coming from his head. I just stood over him and started praying. He was still alive and people gathered around, until eventually a doctor turned up and then the ambulance arrived. I continued to pray for this young man, while Sari spoke to and comforted the driver of the vehicle, who was hysterical. The 18-year-old had been hit on the dual carriageway at 50 mph. Apparently, his friend had called out to him and he had turned round just for a second and hadn't seen the car that was coming straight at him. Being so close to an accident like that affected my life for several days afterwards and I still remember it vividly now. I didn't know what I was doing or what I was praying about at the time. I suppose that is what they call 'standing in the gap'. I found out a few days later, just before we left Northern Ireland, that he had died. Sari and I had to talk it through with some people before we could get our lives back to normal.

We had an assembly at the same school the next morning as a whole team. We decided to shelve what we'd planned and I talked honestly from the heart about God and how important our relationship with him is. It was one of those times where God was present and we were able to pray for the family of this young man. Every young person in school seemed to listen intently to what we had to say, as many of them had also witnessed the accident.

After those two days, it felt as if we'd done ten rounds with Mike Tyson – we were exhausted. It brought home to me then, in my first experience of schools work, that what we do has eternal consequences. But it was also a privilege to be involved in the school at such a difficult and scary time for everyone. It really gave an edge and a focus to the rest of the mission trip. I had an opportunity to get to know the vicar's son of the church that we were staying at – he was into music and Djing like me. We talked a lot and one night he gave me a lift home and, being slightly insensitive like I am sometimes, I thanked him for the lift and opened the car door. But he asked me to wait and talk to him a little bit. He said a couple of sentences then he started to break down and cry. I had the real privilege of leading him back to God after he had walked away from him for a few years. I later found out that after he made that recommitment, he'd also gone away with YWAM but died tragically in a swimming accident. It was a privilege to know him and point him back to God – I will see him again one day.

It would be easy now to say trite comments about why these things happen, but if I am honest, I just don't know why either of those incidents happened. It is still difficult now relaying those stories to you, but the one thing that the media hides from us at all costs is that good can come from bad things. Good can even come from bad choices and good can come from unexplained accidents and incidents. The most personal example that I mentioned before is of my daughters Rhea and Lauren being born seven weeks early, not knowing on a couple of occasions whether they were going to pull through, yet now having 7-year-old twins who are beautiful, full of life and a wonderful gift from God.

Life is a ...

Pete Greig's famous quote is a bit of a surprise to some uptight Christians but I understand where he is coming from. Pete said, 'God is good but life's a bitch.'

Pete said that in the midst of his wife Samie having a brain tumour.[1] Pete also said that 'God is sick and tired of people posing as overcomers with permanent grins as if they somehow managed to dodge the fall and went hanggliding instead.' Sometimes in new church movements it is implied that God wraps us up in bubblewrap, but as you get older you realise that C.S. Lewis had enormous depth when he said, 'we can't have the happiness of yesterday without the pain of today, that's the deal, the pain now is part of the happiness then'.[2]

> So, my son, throw yourself into this work for Christ. Pass on what you heard from me – the whole congregation saying Amen! – to reliable leaders who are competent to teach others. When the going gets

rough, take it on the chin with the rest of us, the way Jesus did. A soldier on duty doesn't get caught up in making deals at the marketplace. He concentrates on carrying out orders. An athlete who refuses to play by the rules will never get anywhere. It's the diligent farmer who gets the produce. Think it over. God will make it all plain.

Fix this picture firmly in your mind: Jesus, descended from the line of David, raised from the dead. It's what you've heard from me all along. It's what I'm sitting in jail for right now – but God's Word isn't in jail! That's why I stick it out here – so that everyone God calls will get in on the salvation of Christ in all its glory. This is a sure thing:

If we die with him, we'll live with him;
If we stick it out with him, we'll rule with him;
If we turn our backs on him, he'll turn his back on us;
If we give up on him, he does not give up –
for there's no way he can be false to himself.

(2 Tim. 2:1–13, The Message)

In a nutshell, Eugene Peterson's wonderful translation says 'Don't give up on life, don't give up on God, God *won't* give up on you'. It astounds me how complicated we make our faith sometimes. Maybe the greatest miracle of all is God bringing good out of bad events. If you look at some persecuted churches across the world, it's astounding that growth comes so readily when hard times are pressing. You wonder whether a bit of persecution might do us good in the Western church – it would certainly move us out of the *Songs of Praise* nicey nice nightmare that the church seems to be stuck in sometimes.

When we were writing this book for guys, we felt it was important that we didn't do the 'ra ra ra we can take the world for Jesus with all smiles and no farting thing'.

It's important that we have a dose of reality when we look at our lives and how we can live them in a better, more godly way. One of the great lessons in life is to realise that sometimes we can't control everything that happens to us in life.

My friends Dave and Susi have shown great faithfulness in particularly difficult times. I asked Dave to share a bit of their story ...

> I've spent a few days trying to work out where to start, and thought the best place was with the me of pre-December 1999. I was married, no kids, worked for the family firm (as a scissor maker). Because my wife and I were in the middle of changing churches, I was taking a break in a course to become a lay reader in the Church of England. We'd moved house to a bigger place the year before, stacking all our financial stability on me. My wife worked as a shop manager in Leeds, which meant travelling from Sheffield every day, and the likelihood of her losing her job was much greater than of me ever losing mine. Late in 1998, things began to change. The scissor firm that I'd hoped to take over when my dad retired went into liquidation, and another company took us over. When I started working for the new company, I was told that my job wouldn't change. It did, and I ended up leaving. I spent a week trying to sell frozen food from the back of a van, before trying my hand as a courier, a white van man. I loved it. The hours could be strange, but I could make more than I'd ever made in my life, and all I had to do was drive. I loved driving, so I found myself in a very good place. Then came December 1999. I can't remember the exact date. You'd think it would be etched in my memory. My first job that morning was

to pick up a load from just off the A57 in Sheffield. Coming up to the roundabout, I was in the outside lane. Straight on at the roundabout, turn right a little way further on, and make the pick-up. As I pulled up to the roundabout, I was shoved violently from behind. I was in a long wheelbase Ford Transit van, and, fortunately, I was wearing a seat belt. The van was pushed out to the centre of the roundabout. This was one of those that are brick-built to a height of around three feet. The van hit it, hard, and the force stopped the van and pitched it sideways, onto the passenger door. I was hanging in mid-air by my seat belt. I radioed back to base that I'd had an accident, a bad one, and then unfastened my safety belt and felt the first shock of pain as I stood up on the passenger door. Within 30 minutes I was in hospital, waiting for an X-ray, but knowing, because everyone told me, that my back had been broken. All I knew back then was that I couldn't deal with that. I liken it to playing pass-the-parcel. I was given a parcel saying 'broken back', took one look and said, 'I can't cope with that God, you have it.' Sounds religious, I know, but I couldn't handle it. I hoped that God would.

Lots of things have happened since, too many to share all, but I'll share a few. I was in hospital for six days before being sent home. My back needed to become stable before they could decide what to do. As I said earlier, all our finances were stacked on me, and when I became disabled (17 per cent according to the government), a downhill spiral started. I know that some people say that you can claim a lot from the government when you know how to work the system. Believe me, even if you're genuine it's not always possible. We always seemed to fall into the cracks that meant we couldn't claim this or that. We knew we couldn't survive financially on the money we had coming in, so we prayed about it. Within a few days, my wife was offered the management of another store, along with the one she already managed. This meant one or two days in Leeds, the others in York. Certainly an answer to prayer, but also the start of more problems.

I was forced to sit at home, unable to help, as I watched my wife leave for work at six in the morning, and return home at nine in the evening, knowing that there was nothing I could do to help. I tried not to let her see how down it was making me. I was upbeat when she came home, but the hours she was away were awful. Of course, when she came home, all she wanted to do was eat and sleep. I was desperate to talk, to spend time with her. She was too tired. After some time, we realised that she couldn't do it anymore. My wife was working all the hours she could, worrying about looking after me. I'd had an operation, the final throw of the medical dice. Unfortunately, a bad outcome meant I was now 20 per cent disabled.

As I write this, it's almost two years since my wife took the job in Sheffield. So where am I now? Well, we now have a car. I re-applied for and have been granted Disability Living Allowance, and that has meant we can afford a car (with a loan from my parents as a down payment). Also, we renegotiated the mortgage, which helped. It meant we could live on my wife's wages and what the government allow me. The fact that I'm 20 per cent (or one-fifth) disabled doesn't sound much, but imagine losing a leg. That's about one fifth of your body. I've lost the use of my back. I can walk 100 yards or so before I have to stop because the pain is too much. I have to use a wheelchair for longer distances. I used to notice the feeling that my legs were going to give way under me. Now that's so normal when I walk, that I hardly notice it anymore.

It's been over two years since I started on the pills for depression, and I still haven't managed to reduce the dose at all. The doctor said that the best thing to help depression was to change what happened to cause it. Not really possible for me. Almost six years on from the accident, and things seem to have become worse. I keep waiting for the light at the end of the tunnel. I wasn't told when I became a Christian that tunnels could be this long. There have been good things happen in those years, but they're hard to see through all the bad. I'm constantly thankful for Susi. I know a lot of marriages would have collapsed under the strain of this. How she copes, I don't know. All I can do is watch as she tackles everything from knitting me jumpers to lifting heavy furniture round. It's stuff like that that hurts most. She has to do stuff I should be doing but can't.

I will start to attend church again. I haven't been able to go since having a panic attack there, but now is the right time to start. It's all small, small steps. Here's to the next one not being too far off.

Please pray for Dave and Susi as they continue to make the best out of a difficult situation. Sometimes there are no easy answers but God is faithful to us even when it is difficult to see it.

I am really glad to know people who have had to struggle through life. I met my uncle Ian (who is really my step uncle but everyone has forgotten) when I was a kid – we played a lot of golf together and he took all the cousins out often to play golf. We always thought he had a bit of a funny walk but we could never quite work out why. In the next few years it became clear that Ian had Multiple Sclerosis (MS) and has been living with it ever since. MS is a strange condition that seems to lie dormant for ages and then accelerate. Ian continues to live with my aunty Jan and my cousin Marc at home. He has his good days and his bad days. I love Ian, Jan and Marc for sticking in there and making the best of what is a difficult situation. Real faithfulness. Ian continues to comment on the world, golf and Sunderland football club and his new found hobby, becoming a computer genius. It is a great community in Billingham. Where Ian lives, he is able to be accepted, helped and loved by the people around them, including their church. It's a great strength of the north east – there is real love and reality in their faith and life, which sometimes I haven't seen in other areas of the country.

> Though the fig tree does not bud
> > and there are no grapes on the vines,
> > though the olive crop fails
> > and the fields produce no food,
> > though there are no sheep in the pen
> > and no cattle in the stalls,
> yet I will rejoice in the Lord,
> > I will be joyful in God my Saviour.
> The Sovereign Lord is my strength;
> > he makes my feet like the feet of a deer,
> > he enables me to go on the heights.
>
> (Hab. 3:17–19, NIV)

Often what is important is how we engage with suffering. In the book *Following Jesus* (Dave Roberts, Relevant Books, 2004), there is a story of a church leader, his son and a not-completely-reformed new convert:

> I spent two years trying to help a former drug dealer grow in faith. He was abusive and manipulative, but could appear deeply spiritual when he wanted to. I would close and stand in front of the doors so he couldn't run out when confronted about his outspoken attacks on individuals in public or his disturbing verbal attacks on his wife. I would be

assaulted by doubt over my handling of him, even after he had sworn at me in public places or lied to me with no sign of remorse. He seduced a woman in our church and eventually left town to a sigh of collective relief among the local churches. I felt like a failure … I had seen the crestfallen anguish and hurt cross someone's face when they were verbally abused. When this man degrades his wife, I fought the urge to give him the right fist of fellowship. I had contained my own mirth when one of my sons, unschooled in spiritual etiquette at the age of four had given him a sharp blow in the groin as he shouted at me. It was followed by a warning to not shout at me again … I had always been aware of my shortcomings but unaware of the pain others carried, I had witnessed it first hand … I had learnt from my life experiences and continued to do so to this day. Think of following Jesus as being like constructing a jigsaw puzzle. The Bible is your guide picture, the jigsaw is your life, be patient with yourself as you put the picture together it takes a long obedience.

Seeing obedience in someone really makes your faith more real

A couple of years ago, I was invited to go with my friend Andy Atkinson as he had been nominated for an award for his volunteer youth work. I first met Andy at Leeds P.H.A.B. club (Physically Handicapped and Able Bodied club). I used to see him every Friday night and played football with him only realising after a few weeks that I couldn't actually foul him because he had two false legs! I still have the lumps on my legs as proof of his 'unique football skills'. Andy was born with severe physical handicaps which left him in need of two artificial legs and a false arm. 'With his disability, he was desperate to fit in and be accepted through being willing to steal from shops and take bikes from the area to gain acceptance with one of the local gangs. Andy's teenage criminal activity escalated until at the age of 21 he was found guilty of car theft and sentenced to a short term in Armley prison in Leeds. Andy, shocked by his prison experience decided to make the best that he could of his life; he started to volunteer for youth work and got involved in running a local football team (I did the disco for them once). He suddenly realised that community and youth work was a way out of some of his struggles.'[3]

Weird church

I have known Andy for many years and talked to him about God often but church was alien to him. He once told me that after I had invited him to a church social event we had on one night, he decided to come along, taking three buses all the way across Leeds, but when he got to the door of the church he looked inside and thought 'These aren't my kind of people'. He went back on his three buses all the way home again. I never even realised he got to the door of the church. I rang him the next day and he said, 'It's just not my thing, these people are different to me' (and he wasn't talking about his disability). It made me think about how church looks to the outside world.

Then our church started meeting for a while in a really rough pub just a few hundred yards from his house, so I invited Andy one night as we worshipped and prayed 'in a pub style'. Andy came along and he met God there one night. When we were having a beer afterwards, he said to me, 'Something has just happened to me, Lee. I just feel like something inside of me has changed as I was singing that song.' Andy made his first steps and he got talking to my mate Toby and others around church. He is still a part of our church community and now does amazing volunteer youth work all across the city of Leeds helping us in schools, and doing Space youth groups and Kidz Klub Leeds and all sorts of different activities.[4] Andy is a real hero, but life for him not only hasn't been easy because of his disability but also due to other things that have happened in his family. Several of his close family ended up in prison for armed robbery and they fell out with Andy. A close member of his family beat him up, degrading him further by using his artificial limbs to beat him in broad daylight. Then his house was set alight by someone close to him. It has been a tough ride for Andy but his obedience to God has been an inspiration for a lot of people.

All those things thrown at Andy, his disability, family trauma, and good still came out of it somehow as he battled through and continued to live his life. It is so healthy to meet people like Andy who have felt suffering at a severe level yet still fought through. It is much more refreshing than the kind of Christianity that somehow avoids the idea of suffering or, just as bad, is obsessed by the idea of suffering and doesn't bring in the hope of the resurrection that God has given us. There must be a balance of handling suffering and celebration to be had somewhere?

I have genuinely heard people say in church, 'Come to know Jesus and everything will be fine', or 'Your life will be all sorted'. That was *never* the guarantee that Jesus gave us, yet somehow we seem to have added that one on quietly.

The following famous bit of the Bible was an amazing comfort to me as I chewed it over (or meditated on it!) for months during a particularly tough time in my life.

> When Jesus saw his ministry drawing huge crowds, he climbed a hillside. Those who were apprenticed to him, the committed, climbed with him. Arriving

at a quiet place, he sat down and taught his climbing companions. This is what he said:

'You're blessed when you're at the end of your rope. With less of you there is more of God and his rule.

'You're blessed when you feel you've lost what is most dear to you. Only then can you be embraced by the One most dear to you.

'You're blessed when you're content with just who you are – no more, no less. That's the moment you find yourselves proud owners of everything that can't be bought.

'You're blessed when you've worked up a good appetite for God. He's food and drink in the best meal you'll ever eat.

'You're blessed when you care. At the moment of being "care-full", you find yourselves cared for.

'You're blessed when you get your inside world – your mind and heart – put right. Then you can see God in the outside world.

'You're blessed when you can show people how to cooperate instead of compete or fight. That's when you discover who you really are, and your place in God's family.

'You're blessed when your commitment to God provokes persecution. The persecution drives you even deeper into God's kingdom.

'Not only that – count yourselves blessed every time people put you down or throw you out or speak lies about you to discredit me. What it means is that the truth is too close for comfort and they are uncomfortable. You can be glad when that happens – give a cheer, even! – for though they don't like it, I do! And all heaven applauds. And know that you are in good company. My prophets and witnesses have always gotten into this kind of trouble.

(Mt. 5:1–12, The Message)

Art or science?

I often discuss with DJs and musicians whether DJing is an art or a science. The answer is probably that it is a bit of both. There are certain technical skills that we have, but there is also an art in blending records, scratching and making sounds unique. Our faith is very similar, there is an art and science to it. Some things are just fact and are unchanging, yet with some things, we need to be creative. We need to find a balance between the art and the science, and the celebration and the suffering. They are part of the same package.[5]

Questions

- What is suffering?
- Did people in the Bible suffer?
- Which story in this chapter has been most moving for you?
- Howe do you handle the bad times and who gets the blame.
- How can bad stuff be used by God?

Notes

[1] You can read more about Pete and Samie's story in the book *Red Moon Rising*, Kingsway Publications, 2004.
[2] From the film *Shadowlands*, Spelling Films International, 1993.
[3] From 'Faithworks News' issue 2, Dave Vann. Used with kind permission www.faithworks.info
[4] See www.networkleeds.com
[5] Even while writing this chapter I have had several conversations with people I know who have told me about amazing struggles they are having to learn to deal with in their lives, yet all these people are getting on with life and God is using them in amazing ways. Is this, as the comedian John Archer puts it, a 'pair-of-ducks' (paradox)?

God give me strength to face a fact though it slay me.

(Thomas H. Huxley, 1825–1895)

27

Paraskavedekatriaphobia

BAZ GASCOYNE

One crisp Monday morning 25 years ago, I was travelling from Darlington to Bishop Auckland telephone exchange with a colleague from British Telecom. The sun was shining, my colleague was happy listening to his jazz tape and I was drifting in and out of some daydream. Suddenly, the brakes screeched and the car came to a sudden halt. 'What's up?" I asked.

'The magpie,' he replied.

'What about it?' I asked. 'Did you hit it?'

'No, there's only one.'

'So?'

'Well, I can't go on until we see its partner.'

'What?'

'It's unlucky to only see one magpie. We'll have to wait until we see the second one.'

So five minutes passed and we're sat still so that my colleague, a man in his fifties, a husband and father, can see a second magpie so that we could continue on our journey.

Over 15 minutes later and we were still at the side of the road. Eventually it appeared. My colleague smiled, suggested to me it wasn't that bad waiting, started the engine and drove away from two magpies who appeared to be grinning in our direction.

Superstitions have been passed down from generation to generation in many families and many nations, if not all. My gran was quite superstitious and was adamant not to let me pass her on the stairs or clean my shoes on the table as this would bring bad luck.

Interestingly, I myself was superstitious when it came to playing sports. I would always put on my kit, be it football, rugby or athletics, in the same way. Always my shorts first, followed by my left shin-pad if wearing them, followed by left sock, then left boot and then I'd put on all of the right side gear followed by the shirt. Even when I had been on the losing side one week I would still go through the routine the following week. What a sad case I was, thinking this would help instead of realising it was to do with ability and team-mates.

So, superstition has been around for hundreds of years and has come from many different avenues including the church, presumably because people centuries ago didn't have the understanding of the natural world that we have today. The dictionary states that superstition is 'an unfounded belief that some action or circumstance completely unrelated to a course of events can influence its outcome'.

In England, we like to think that we are logical but many of our traditions derive from superstitions. For instance, when someone sneezes we Brits will say 'Bless you' as it's the polite thing to say, while the Germans say 'Gesundheit!'. This tradition goes right back to the great plagues of Europe, when anyone who began sneezing violently was almost certain of death. The Pope of that time passed a law requiring people blessed the sneezer as well as requiring the sneezer to cover their mouth with a cloth or their hand. This was to try and stop the disease. However, many believed that it was to keep the soul intact, as sneezing into the air would allow the soul to escape, which would soon mean death for the person. So people had to call on God's blessing for that person.

In 2004, according to www.luckfactor.co.uk/survey.html, 4,000 people in Britain took part in an Internet survey. The purpose was to determine whether they thought they were lucky or unlucky and if they were superstitious.

Interestingly, the report reveals that people who think they are lucky make sure they act out superstitious behaviour to experience good luck, whereas the people who believe they are unlucky believe it is down to their belief of superstitions that brings them bad luck.

The survey found that the following were the top superstitions with the percentage of the 4,000 who endorsed each one.

Touching wood	86%
Crossing fingers	64%
Walking under a ladder	49%
Breaking a mirror	34%
Worried about the number 13	25%
Carrying a lucky charm	24%

(www.luckfactor.co.uk/survey.html)

It seems clear that we are a pretty superstitious nation, but what is interesting is where many of these superstitions came from, with many originating from the church.

Let as look at some of the most popular superstitions and why and how the church introduced them into society.

Friday 13th

This is also known as 'Paraskavedekatriaphobia'. One of the reasons given for Friday 13th being considered unlucky is that there were 13 people at the last supper of Jesus, the thirteenth person entering the room being Judas who betrayed Jesus, and, Jesus was crucified on a Friday – Good Friday, as it's known. Good for whom? Certainly not Jesus but definitely for you and me.

According to an article by Dr Dossey, between 17–21 million Americans suffer from Paraskavedekatriaphobia and up to 4–5 million here in the UK (www.drdossey.com/fri13.htm). He tells his patients that once they can pronounce 'Paraskavedekatriaphobia' they are cured. I'm sure that if you said it fast enough a few times it could sound like speaking in tongues and you might even get an interpretation!

Walking under a ladder

There are various records behind why this was originally considered to be unlucky. When the ladder is leaning against the wall it forms the shape of a triangle, which was used centuries ago as the symbol of the Holy Trinity. By walking under a ladder, you were violating the big three. Another reason was that it used to be a method of execution and men who were hung were hung from the seventh rung of a ladder leaning against a tree. In this case, being under the ladder was definitely not a good place to be!

Crossing fingers

The belief here was that if you make the sign of the Christian faith with your fingers, evil spirits would be prevented from destroying our chances of good fortunes.

One magpie

One understanding is that a magpie was originally an evil crow. Evil because it did not wear its full mourning dress for the death of Christ! Also, if you salute the magpie it dilutes the evil.

If you want to see an in-depth list of superstitions please check out www.oldsuperstitions.com.

Health warning

Please be warned: if you have a tendency to be superstitious you might not want to carry on with your life after reading all the different beliefs people have about things to bring good or bad luck. If you do, you could well be afraid to wash, wink, wee, walk but almost definitely worry!

It's possible that after reading the previous pages or checking out the website you have had a good snigger to yourself wondering how anyone could believe that behaving a certain way could affect how their day or life unfolds.

Well, can I ask you to ask yourself right now the following question: Do I have any superstitions in my life? It could be to do with your relationships, work, sports, or even with your walk with God if you are a follower of Jesus. Hello? Now who's laughing? It is so easy to get into things which become superstitions without realising that they are.

So why a chapter on superstitions in a book that's talking about men's walk with God? I believe that in many areas of our church life we can end up being superstitious about certain aspects and lose the real meaning. Rather than 'getting life' from aspects of church life, and our relationship with God being enhanced, they can become superstitions, or ties, which bring only frustration, fear and death in our walk with God.

Communion

I used to try so hard to get a mental picture of Jesus hanging on the cross. Try to see his beaten, bloody body struggling and gasping for a breath while I would take the bread and wine. Most Sundays, if not all, I would fail and then feel guilty for not being able to do so. I thought it was about picturing what he went through so I could generate suitably solemn thoughts. Instead of taking communion to remember what Jesus had done for me and leaving thankful that he took my anger, lust, jealousy, hatred, gossiping, bitterness, envy and judgemental behaviour (all my sin) when he was crucified so that I could be free and begin a new life forgiven and living the way God intended me to, I would leave church after taking the bread and wine frustrated, down and worse than when I had arrived. Why does it have to be such a solemn occasion when Jesus said 'do this in remembrance of me'? Surely that means all his life, birth, walking on this earth, the miracles he performed, and the lives changed, yes his death but also the fantastic resurrection of his life. Now I can get excited about that and enjoy taking communion with a grateful heart. Be sombre, or ecstatically happy, or both, but let's not tie ourselves into a tortuous 'must feel' tradition that's not real.

Reading the Bible

What, are you saying reading the Bible is a superstition, Baz? No, I'm not saying that, but it can so easily become like reading your horoscope or playing bingo! When I first became a Christian, I was so excited about reading the

Bible that I would faithfully read it alongside my *Daily Bread* Bible notes. My mother was not over keen on my new found faith in God. I can understand that having seen me six months earlier in hospital having my stomach pumped after taking a cocktail of pills and alcohol, she probably thought I was going mad. So, to try and keep the peace in the house, I used to hide my Bible notes inside the middle of a book entitled *The Man in the Iron Mask*. I had cut the middle pages out with a Stanley knife and slotted the notes inside. I am sure she knew, just like I knew she hid the biscuits in the washer from my brother and me. I will ask her next time I see her ...

My Bible was an old King James version which I had been presented with when I was at junior school. Initially, reading the Bible was exciting as I wanted to discover more about Father God and Jesus and the way I was to live my life. But over the years I have seen myself reading the Bible for lots of different reasons, not always good. At times, I have read it not for my own benefit but because I have been worried about what others would think if I hadn't read it for a few days, weeks or months. So I would read begrudgingly to appease my conscience. At other times, I thought that if I did not read it God would stop loving me.

And how many of us have fallen into the trap of 'unless I read my Bible today I will have a bad day'? Where does that sound familiar? 'Scorpio, you need to make sure you have a clean pair of knickers just in case!'

And what about Bible bingo where you just open it and hope that God will speak? That is until you do just that then read 'go and be circumcised' and with a grimace close your Bible and your legs.

The other danger is that we read the Bible so that we can look more knowledgeable to others because of our vast understanding and the ability to quote the book and verse, maybe even holding our open Bible low enough so that others can be impressed with all our underlining and highlighting. It's possible to worship and love the Bible more than we do Jesus. Then the Bible moves from being the life-giving word that points to our God, to becoming our god/superstition. I remember once when I felt so intimidated by how well-read other people's Bibles looked compared to mine that I spent 15 minutes throwing mine around, stamping on it trying to make it looked well used!

I love the Bible, as it's the Word of God, but we need to ensure we read it for the right reasons and not as a superstitious back-up to our day.

Prayer

Ever fallen asleep without finishing your prayer with the phrase 'In the name of Jesus. Amen' and then worried when you woke up that the prayer was wasted and God couldn't answer it? Rather than prayer being a discussion between Father and child it can so easily become such a ritual filled with superstition.

Years ago I was praying with a friend of mine called Dave (not his real name) and a leader of a church who insisted we called him 'Pastor'. Well, when the prayers began I thought what the hell is this? In a deep, booming, voice the pastor began, 'O Lord, we just come to you this morning just to ask your blessing, Lord, on Dave as he comes to the end of his time working, Lord, but also as Baz replaces him, Lord.' By this time, I am staring at him wide eyed as I listened to him speak to God in a totally different voice and style to what he did when he talked to anybody else. The prayer finished with an impressive 'in the M–I–G–H–T–Y name of J–E–S–U–S A–MEN!'.

Dave began his prayer, 'Lord, I just thank you, Lord, that we can come to you today, Lord, and just ask for your blessing on Baz, Lord. Lord, what would we do, Lord, without you, Lord, because then we wouldn't be able to come to you, Lord, and ask, Lord, your blessing, Lord, on this work, Lord.' By this time I was definitely in need of the Lord's help as I could feel my shoulders moving as I tried to stop myself breaking out into uncontrollable laughter. Thankfully, I also stopped myself from shouting out at the top of my voice 'STOP for goodness' sake! Just pray! God knows who he is, just pray.' Eventually after another 654 'Lords', 'buts' and 'justs', I heard an 'amen' somewhere. Then it happened: silence, for what seemed like eternity whilst the 'Just Lord Brothers' waited for me to offer up my prayer. Well, it was going to be a long wait as I couldn't pray like a malfunctioning robot. So, eventually the holy shuffle, cough and then hush commenced to indicate that we had finished praying.

Does God only listen when we put our 'prayer voice' on? Is there a Christian prayer style that shows we mean business, or are we convincing ourselves that God will hear us if we put on a good display. I'm not pointing the finger at those guys in particular because we've all done it at times: put on a more impressive voice in the belief that it somehow makes a difference.

When I first became a Christian in 1977, I was encouraged by Peter Nodding, the gentleman who prayed with me on that day, to talk to God as I would talk to my best mate. This is what I have tried to do ever since. I know this at times can sound flippant or like I'm not taking God seriously but surely it must be better to teach people to be real rather than develop a 'secular voice' and a 'prayer voice'? Try to imagine my wife, Linda, telling me she loved me during a romantic and intimate meal: 'Baz, I just want you to know, Baz, how much, Baz, I love you, Baz. Thanks, Baz, for marrying me, because, Baz, if you hadn't, Baz, I wouldn't be here now, Baz, but you are Baz, and I am pleased, Baz, that you are Baz because if you were not Baz who would you be?' If I'd have been feeling turned on before, I would now certainly be sitting on a bucket of ice.

And how easy it is to throw in a few 'Keys for my Sierra', 'Cracker my shin' or 'We'll have a crash man' not to stir our spirits, but because we believe it will make our prayers sound more effective.

I've heard my good friend, Steve, tell us not to try and pray clever prayers, because they've all been said, instead just to pray what's on your heart. Good advice, I'd say.

The Creed and the Lord's Prayer

Some years ago I went to an evening service at an Anglican church back home in Darlington. It was an even song service where they use the 1630 hymn and service book. The service was fantastic as I really had to concentrate on what I was doing, saying and hearing. My friends were very apologetic after the service because of how boring it was. They did not believe me when I told them I loved it and found it very inspiring. They laughed as they thought I was trying to be humorous but I was serious: I had met with God in a way I had not in the style of worship or meeting I was used to. Why? Because I had to engage rather than switch easily onto autopilot – so easy to do when using the same words, songs or music every week, regardless of style.

Prayer and statements can be items of faith or they can be a tradition that have lost their meaning: a ritual that must be completed to appease us.

24/7 *prayer*

What's so amazing about human beings is that we can create superstition and tradition out of something that is radical and new. It has been great to see how God has used the 24/7 prayer movement over recent years. Our church have done numerous weeks, or part-weeks, and seen some great answers to prayer.

Recently, I was chatting with a young lady in our church and we laughed as we talked about how we worry about 'breaking the chain'. How? By talking to the person at the changeover so that there's no one praying for a few minutes, or leaving the prayer room to go and answer the door and let the next person in or the last person out. 'Help, the prayer chain has been broken and God has declared all prayers null and void!'

I laughed with her but recognised that this is how I felt when I and a friend prayed together in our prayer room. We shared our hopes, dreams and fears for about 40 minutes and then prayed together for the last 20 minutes. It was a fantastic time, but in the back of my mind I was thinking, 'We wasted 40 minutes by talking and not praying.' What about the times when we fall asleep during our prayer slot?

How we create stress for ourselves by living as if our walk with God is a series of tasks and constraints to fit into, rather than a relationship. A relationship where we're honest and express our thoughts. Pouring out our thanks, our praise, our adoration, confession, thanksgiving and supplication – but what if we get them in the wrong order? It's good to have a heart of gratitude and express our love for God rather than always rushing into his presence with our requests, but if we have something weighing on our hearts, does he really want us to force ourselves through a ritual of 'Have to thank and praise first, then confess before I can ask' rather than pour out our hearts to him?

Worship leaders

The meeting has begun and the person leading the meeting has prayed, welcomed God and handed over to the worship leader to begin the worship. The worship leader then says, 'Can we just pray?' Is their prayer better than the person who has already prayed so the worship and the meeting will be better? Have they missed out their worship team prayer that morning so think it can't possibly go well unless they put that right, even if it is in front of the whole church? Answers on a postcard or email to www.leeandbaz.com.

The cross

One thing that really gets me shouting at the television is seeing a footballer running onto the pitch, making the sign of the cross as his good luck charm. Why does this agitate me? Because if he is worth between £25–40 million he should not be relying on some superstition of making the sign of the cross to help him play well. The cross is powerful, and the work of the cross is far-reaching, but it isn't a good luck symbol to help us do well in our games of life.

So, probably a few sacred cows being shot in that chapter. Let's not throw out the things of God, but let's remember what they're about and not allow them to become rituals and superstitions with little meaning.

Questions

- In what areas of your life do you act superstitiously?
- Fear is the main source of superstition. So what are you fearful of that makes you superstitious?
- What superstition have you seen in the church?

Nothing is a waste of time if you use the experience wisely.

(Rodin)

28

Get Off the Verge

BAZ GASCOYNE

Agoraphobia, Brontophobia, Hypsiphobia, Myctophobia, Nosocomephobia, Odontophobia, Pteromerhanophobia, Pyrophobia, Thalassophobia and Trypanophobia are phobias that probably you or someone you know has experienced at some time or another.

Unless you have experienced fear of open spaces, thunder and lightning, heights, the dark, hospitals, teeth or dental surgery, flying, fire, sea or injections it is very difficult to empathise with the suffering and torment the individual experiences because of their phobia or phobias.

> Phobias are irrational fears of something that most people are not afraid of, such as spiders, crowds, small spaces or flying. Phobias can cause considerable disruption to life. Phobias affect 4 per cent of men and 13 per cent of women.
>
> (http://hcd2.bupa.co.uk/ fact_sheets/html/phobias.html)

There is one phobia that most, if not all, experience once in their lifetime and that is Atychiphobia. This can be instilled in us whilst we are young or even when we have retired. Atychiphobia? The fear of failure.

The fear of failure can have such a hold on a life that it can affect a person for years. For me it began when I was 10 or 11 years old at school, which I recount in the chapter 'Life or death?'.

Whatever or whoever planted the seed of the fear of failure in your life, or whenever it is first planted, it can have a damaging effect on your life.

I was one of those strange children who just loved school, both junior and senior, and have so many happy memories. I did not suffer from Scolionophobia – a fear of school. However, from the age of 11 I did suffer from Sophophobia (the fear of learning) and Atychiphobia. I became so nervous walking into the classroom and believed I could not and would not learn anything. It was amazing how this affected my life in so many ways.

> I can accept failure, but I can't accept not trying.
>
> (Michael Jordan)

Unfortunately, I was the opposite of this. I was so afraid of failing that probably 98 per cent of the time I would not even try. Sports was no problem as I was quite good at this but anything to do with academia – studying, reading or writing – I became overwhelmed with this great sense of uselessness every time I sat down at a desk. I would try but always with the resounding echo of, 'You will never achieve anything' bouncing around in my mind.

I still have my school report from when I was at senior school which covered the years from 11 to 16. It makes such an interesting read. Mainly Cs and apart from B+ every year for PE (physical education) my position in the exam results most reads: 29th out of 34, 10th out of 13, or 30th out of 36 (so mostly below average). The only good thing about my report, which still makes me laugh out loud every time I look at it, is the wallpaper used to back the report.

My ex-stepdad came home once after drinking all day, and decided that he would decorate the front room, known as the sitting room. Why it was called the sitting room I'll never know as it was the one room no one was allowed to go and sit in. It was more like a museum – it was there but no one went in it! So because of the regular earful from my mother about the room needing re-decorating, he began the task of wallpapering the whole room even though he was under the influence of alcohol.

What makes me laugh is that after he had finished and tidied the room back to what it was like before he then called us all in to admire his work. We walked past a proud man as we walked into an immaculate room. My brother and I thought that he had done a brilliant job but my mother kept saying, 'Something does not look right, but I can't work out what it is.'

As my mother continued to look at the paper on the wall, she asked if there were any rolls of the paper left. The one remaining unopened roll of paper was produced and carefully opened to reveal the problem: 'You bloody idiot, you have hung all the paper upside down.'

After deciding the pattern looked upside down, he had painstakingly unrolled every roll then rolled them back the way he thought they should be. You have to admire his commitment. So he had hung the paper the correct way according to his 20/20 vision produced by the infamous Newcastle Brown Ale. Fortunately, because no one was allowed to sit in the sitting room, only the four of us knew what had happened but it has caused many a hilarious memory since.

Anyway, the report that this same wallpaper provided a cover for, was pretty much the story through and through. Once I had left school, my fear of failure continued to hinder me in the big wide world. I went to the local technical college to do a catering course but left after four weeks as I could not cope with a female version of Gordon Ramsay telling me I was useless in a high Scottish accent. So I went to sixth form college to join my friends but spent most of the time in the common room listening to the jukebox, playing pool and table football. Eventually, I was asked to leave by the principal. I could come up with so many excuses for why I did not stick these courses out but it was all down to the fear of failure.

I got a job and enjoyed it until studying at night school became part of the deal. I always stopped attending once the light nights kicked in. I always used the excuse that I was needed to play football but again it was down to the fear of taking exams and failing.

In 1981, I went to Cliff College, the Methodist Bible College near Sheffield. Once again my fear raised its ugly head. Alongside my course, I decided to take some O levels so I signed up to do English Language and Religious Education.

In the lectures, I would sit at the back of the lecture theatre and try to listen and concentrate but mostly I would feel a sense of failure and believing the lie 'You will never achieve anything'. It took me three months to pluck up enough courage to ask one of the lecturers what 'NIV' stood for. He replied kindly, 'The New International Version of the Bible' and I tried to ignore the stares and looks of disgust from some of my fellow students. Interestingly though, I did have about eight out of the eighty come up to me afterwards and thank me as they had not known either, but hadn't dared to ask!

The day of my RE exam arrived and I sat for about an hour with a totally blank mind, consumed by fear, not writing a single word. Eventually, I got up from my seat, walked to the front of the room and handed my exam paper in. The invigilator looked at it and asked, 'Have you finished?'

'Yes,' I replied.

He looked at the paper: 'You haven't done anything.'

'I can't,' I replied and left the room once again feeling such a failure.

Even though I knew God had changed my life for the better I did not believe or think I would ever experience what we read in Mk. 10:27: 'For with God all things are possible (NKJV).'

I wondered if I would ever be free from this curse on my life. This was my Goliath for which I needed God's help to face head on and conquer once and for all.

> For though a righteous man falls seven times, he rises again ...
>
> (Prov. 24:16, NIV)

> I am convinced that God is more pleased with those who step out and fail than those who sit back and do nothing out of fear of failure.
>
> (Larry Tomczak, *Divine Appointments*,
> Kingsway Publications Ltd, 1987)

I knew this is what I had to do to break the pattern. I had taken my English O level three times and failed three times in 1979, 1982 and 1985. So 22 years on from leaving senior school, I enrolled at Sheffield Norton College to do English Language and Literature every Tuesday morning for approximately 36 weeks.

One morning I was driving to a school that I visit regularly when on the radio Nicky Campbell was interviewing an author about his latest book and taking phone calls from people who wanted to ask the author questions. One caller's question and the author's reply really grabbed my attention and I believed God was trying to make a point to me. The caller wanted to know how to go about writing a book he was thinking about. Immediately, the author interrupted with something like 'Easy. Stop thinking about it and get off the verge and do it.' He just kept saying get off the verge, get off the verge. Then Nicky Campbell got really animated as he suggested that this should be the motto for every person in the country thinking about doing something. 'Get off the verge, just get off the verge.' I think the caller had got the message, as had I. 'Get off the verge and do something.'

This is what I had done by enrolling for the course. I was determined not to let a lie ruin my life any longer.

When I arrived at the college on that first day, I was nervous and fearful but determined to push through and begin to break this fear with God's help. I was one of about 23 students, some mature like myself returning to study, others who had just recently left school. Interestingly, by the end of the course only the dozen or so mature students were left, me included. I loved the course. Yes, it was difficult, stretching and demanding at times but I read books by authors I had never heard of. I read modern poetry, Thomas Hardy, I studied Macbeth which was brilliant. I loved the fact that our tutor loved what she did and brought it alive. Every so often I would battle with the inner demons of 'Go home why are you bothering? You will never achieve anything' but I persevered, encouraged by my tutor. As the year came to an end we approached the exam dates. All the bad memories of the past came rushing back, but the exams came and went and soon I received my letter. It informed me that I had passed with a B and A. I had to read it numerous times for the truth to sink in. Had they made a mistake? Had I got someone else's results by mistake or had I really passed? When the certificate arrived through the post I knew I had really passed.

And so, in September 2000, I began a part time Master of Arts degree at Cliff College and Sheffield University in Evangelism Studies. This was a huge step from GSCE English Language and Literature and as the day for the first semester approached I could feel the fear trying to raise its ugly head again.

Well, Monday 11 September was upon me and after lots of hugs, kisses and words of encouragement like 'you can do this, Baz' I drove to the college. Once there, I sat in the car park feeling excited but far more nervous and apprehensive, watching people arrive and walk confidently into the centre, intelligence oozing out of them. All that was oozing out of me was nervous wind! It took me about 15 minutes to get enough courage to get out and walk to the centre. I could feel myself slowly disappearing down the plughole of fear of failure and learning. I was now walking around the building and after my third circuit I shouted at God 'Please help me get in there!'

The reply I got was quite a shock to me, 'Get yourself in there then I will look after you.' Basically, God was saying 'trust me'. As Murphy Tobin said:

> Trust is the antidote for fear. Trust that we will be given everything we need to get through this moment and this day.
>
> (Murphy Tobin)

So in I walked, up the stairs and into the room where we were to have our lectures. There were about 25 people already in the room. I immediately headed for the back where I belonged. The lecturer introduced himself and said that we were going to have a time together worshipping God and praying. As the worship began and people were standing and singing I began to feel very insecure and told God so.

Once again he said to me, 'I will look after you and help you through this course, trust me.' I turned into a male version of Vicki Pollard: 'No but yeah but yeah but yeah no but yeah no but yeah … but no because I'm useless.'

God then asked, 'Where are you?' I could feel myself getting angry and replied, 'God, I know where I am. I am in a room full of swots and I'm feeling very uncomfortable and also annoyed with you and these stupid questions.'

'No, Baz, look around. Where are you?'

'I am sat on a brown plastic chair at the back of a room surrounded by twenty-plus others who all look clever sods. Happy now?'

'No,' came his response. 'Look where you are sat on the brown plastic chair, Baz.' So I looked around whilst the others were sat, stood or kneeling, worshipping God. As I continued to span the room realisation kicked in.

'Oh my word, God, I now understand what you are trying to get through to me.' BINGO. It was one of those Mcfly moments, God knocking, asking if there was anyone home. It was a red letter day. What God was trying very patiently to show me was that I was sat in the very spot where I became a Christian 23 years earlier in July of 1977.

With my heart pounding, lips quivering and tears streaming down my cheeks I got off my chair and lay flat out on the carpet. God had certainly got my attention. He had shown me that he had helped me this far through the ups and downs of my life so he could help me through the next two years. I could not control myself emotionally as I lay there trying to thank God in between the deep gasps for breath and the sobbing, sniffing, shaking, stuttering sentences of thanks. Silence began to fall in the room apart from my Morse code of crying as the first semester began. I eventually picked myself up from the floor and sat back in my chair and I was off once again trying to be studious.

All the way through the two years, God was true to his word. I did not always find it easy doing the assignments or trying to read or study books I needed to, but God kept on coming through. The following two semesters he just reminded me of his promise. Both times I collected a key for my room I was to discover that I was staying in my old college rooms that I had had when I was a full-time student at the college in 1981 and 1984. Once again, I was left in tears due to God's faithfulness. Each assignment came and went and I managed to scrape through. Even when I would feel down and be struggling with the workload whilst I continued to work full time and end up shouting from the office in our attic to my wife, 'I can't do this!' she would encouragingly shout back, 'Shut up! Of course you can, just get on with it.'

All the assignments were done and all my research complete for the 20,000 word dissertation. Linda had typed it up and I delivered it to the binders on Christmas Eve. I felt a huge weight lifted off as I went into Christmas and New Year. All I had to do now was wait for the result of my dissertation.

In February, I received an email from the college informing me that my dissertation had failed by one mark. Well, me, not the dissertation. I had failed. Once again I felt such a failure. I was so angry. One sodding mark; I could not believe it. As is the tendency with me, I reacted straight away and emailed Martyn, the postgraduate tutor, immediately saying something like, 'Stuff it, I tried my best and I am not going to resubmit my dissertation. I will just have the Postgraduate Diploma rather than the MA. Thanks. Baz.'

When Linda arrived home from work, I informed her of what had happened and of my decision. Don't you just love it when people really know you? Her reply was, 'OK love, if that's what you want to do.' It wasn't what I wanted to do it but I was angry and feeling sorry for myself. I was having a pity party and wanted her to join in with me. As usual, once I had calmed down three days later, Linda and I could talk about how I was really feeling and what I wanted to do – which was work on the dissertation, resubmit it and obtain the Master of Arts degree.

So I humbly emailed Martyn to apologise for my outburst and inform him that I would like to resubmit my dissertation.

> Life shrinks or expands in proportion to one's courage.
>
> (Anais Nin (1903–77))

The only downside to having to resubmit, was that I would not be able to graduate the same day as my friends from my year. After listening to what I did wrong, rewriting about 10,000 words and using the data I collated to better my argument and evaluation, I felt quietly confident as I handed in the finished dissertation to the college a few months later.

Once again, I had to wait to discover whether I would be celebrating or being consoled. At the age of 43, I received the news that I had obtained a Masters degree. I had conquered my fear of learning and failure in the whole area of studying, something that had restricted me and caused me so much heartache over the years.

> If you don't risk anything you risk even more.
>
> (Erica Jong)

I have found it easy to relate to David and some of his struggles in the Bible. He was a man who was honest and wore his heart on his sleeve about his fears.

> My heart is in anguish within me. Stark fears over-
> power me. Trembling and horror overwhelm me.
> Oh, for wings like a dove, to fly away and rest. I
> would fly to the far off deserts and stay there. I
> would flee to some refuge from this storm.
>
> (Ps. 55:4–8, The Living Bible)

We need to have a sense of reality in our prayers to God.
As a man, it's important that you feel you can say whatever
you want to God. When we are honest God meets us at
our place of honesty. During my journey with God, I have
often shouted and sworn in anger, full of bitterness and
even hatred to him, to do with the way I felt about feeling
like a failure.

Well, 13 September 2003, I sat with hundreds of other
students in Sheffield University Octagon Centre waiting
for the graduation ceremony to begin. Sat in the bleachers
was my beautiful wife Linda and my mother along with
many other proud loved ones of the students waiting to
receive their certificates. As my name was called out and I
walked onto the stage in my cap and gown, I punched the
air as I walked up to the university professor who would
shake my hand and congratulate me on my achievement.
I knew this was not the end but the beginning of pushing
through the things that had held me back. Facing fears so
that I can become the best Baz Gascoyne that God wants
me to be and is helping me to become.

> Our lives improve only when we take chances and
> the first and most difficult risk we can take is to be
> honest with ourselves.
>
> (Walter Anderson, http://
> www.quotationspage.com/subjects/risk)

Questions

- In what areas of your life are you ruled by a fear or fears?
- Today, are you prepared to admit this to yourself or someone you trust so that you can begin to walk into the freedom that God has for you?
- In what area of your life do you need to 'get off the verge'?

In the end there has to be hope.

(Douglas Coupland)